PASSAGES

PASSAGES

POEMS 1969–2019

Paul Rossiter

ISOBAR
PRESS

First published in 2024 by

Isobar Press
Sakura 2-21-23-202, Setagaya-ku,
Tokyo 156-0053, Japan

&

14 Isokon Flats, Lawn Road,
London NW3 2XD, United Kingdom

https://isobarpress.com

ISBN 978-4-907359-49-2

COVER IMAGE: Wilhelmina Barns-Graham, *Untitled (white circle series)*, Nov–Dec 2002, acrylic on paper © Wilhelmina Barns-Graham Trust. Back cover author photograph by Mayako Murai.

INTERIOR IMAGES: Page 48, photograph of Plumgarths Bungalow, Kendal, by Yoko Tsuruta. Page 302, J. B. Guilbert, *Vue de l'amphithéatre d'Arles* (Musée départemental de l'Arles antique). Photographs of Al Fintas, Mt Oku Hotaka-dake, Borobudur, Jomsom, and Kyōdō by Paul Rossiter.

for Maya

CONTENTS

ONE (1969)

I

Seafarer   24
Bashō   27

TWO (1969–1978)

II

Reading the T'ang Poets in Tokyo, 1969   38
Club Mugen   39
Angkor   40
Jantar Mantar Observatory   41
Bare Rock   42
Alpine   43
Climbing Rock   44
Uses of the Seashore   47

III

E. P. Young and Old   50
Visiting Wei Pa after Twenty Years (*after Tu Fu*)   51
Mad Song   52
The Poem, Almost   53
Vernacular   54
On Trevose Head   55
In the Mountains: Four Poems   56
In the Mountains: Five Days   58
Wythburn Valley   60
Musica Universalis   62
Wintering   63

Hebridean   64
Gulf Stream   65
Crossing the Pass   66
Stramongate Bridge 1 a.m.   67
The Gate   68

IV

Hearing the Black-Throated Divers Call   70
Looking at the Work Ken Wall Does   74
Snow Falling and Then Stopping   76
Hitchhiking to Cornwall, Paying Two Visits, and
          Hitchhiking Back Again   78

V

Seeing Sights in Sanctuary Wood   84
The Temptation of St Anthony   86

THREE (1978–1981)

VI

The Dancer and the Dance   92
Attention   95
Nightclub Work   96
Market   97
Covent Community Garden   98
Crystal   99
Birds of a Feather   100
W. S. 1611   102
Ariel   103
Pizza Apocalittica   104

Les Saltimbanques de Westbourne Park   106
10th August 1979   108
About a Marriage   110
Funeral   111
Seeing Kung-sun's Pupil Dance *(Tu Fu)*   112
Wang Wei Writes a Letter   114
A Panel from the Cathedral Door   115
Lunch Break in the Park   116
The Tramp   118

VII

Limeuil   120
Valley Morning   121
Greetings   122
Husbandry   124

VIII

Paradeisos   126
Art Pepper in London   128
Rhyme   129
Cage & Cunningham   130
Cerne Abbas   132
Avebury   136
Empires   137
Sparrow   138

IX

Altitude   144
Waking   145
Al Fintas   146
Mina Al-Ahmadi, North Pier   147
Desert Sun, Wind from the North   148
Reading Horace in Kuwait   150
In the Emirate   153

The Question of Palestine   154
Cairo   155
The Favours   156
In the Tomb of Rameses VI   158
Palaeopaphos   159
Monastery in Cyprus   161
Meltemi   162

FOUR (1981–1991)

X

On Arrival   166
Tokyo: Weeks One & Two   170
Komachi   172
Straw Against the Winter   174
Zuisenji Garden   176
All That Flows   177
Zazen for Foreigners   178
Visiting Ian in Prison   179
In Izu   180
In Izu (2)   181
Glimpsing the Garden   182
Sanjūsangen-dō   183
Four Postcards from Kyoto   184
Kogō, Scene 2   187
The Old Man of Shimo-Ochiai   190
Bashō: Haiku   191
Some Cultural Uncertainties   192
Air   193
Climbing, Descending   194
Changing, Unchanged   198
Bon-Odori in Kabukichō   199
Bow, Clap Twice, and Pray   200

XI

Hōkokuji   202
The Way of Tea   204
Kagekiyo   205
Hiroshima   208
Ifu Beach, Kumejima   210
From the Train   212
The Old Lady of Ogikubo   213
Language Acquisition   214
Sashimi and Roses   215
Vacuum Storm (*Natsuishi Ban'ya*)   216

.XII

Monumenta Nipponica   220
The Four Seasons in Tokyo   226

FIVE (1983–1995)

XIII

The Blue Edge   234
Beach   236
Poseokjeong Bower   237
Ginseng Wine with Mr Kwon   238
Watching the World Lightweight Championship on TV
     While Eating Dinner in a Bulgogi Restaurant in
     Kyongju with Chirone   239
Three Stone Buddhas   240
The Kingdom of Pagan   241
Petals and Grace Notes   242
The Waves   244
Pak Wayan, Sitting on the Veranda of His Losmen   249

Some Roads in Bali 250
How to Paint the World 251
Kubutambahan 252
Pura Besakih 254
Mount Batur 256
A Dance in Ubud 257
Hall of Justice 258
Borobudur 259
A Courtyard in Bangli 263

XIV

Current Accounts 266
Live from Cairo 269

XV

In the World 272
Hotel Bangkok 273
Gold Rush 274
Ceremony at Ayers Rock 275

XVI

The Burial Mask 280
Love's Labour 281

SIX (1991–2002)

XVII

To Whom It May Concern 288
Eternal Life 289
Trousers 290

Topography   291
A Tragicomedy in Five Acts, Presented to Great Applause   292
Utopia, Arcadia   293
The Small Big Band   294
The Cats   295
Hotel Infinity   296

XVIII

In Arles   298

XIX

Midwinter   306
On Arrival   309
Acqua Alta   310
Miracles   312
La Serenissima   313
Duomo   318
Palazzo Pitti   319
At Fiesole   320
Fonte Gaia   322
The Visit   324
Midwinter Return   325

XX

Branch Line   328
Babble   330
One Way   332
For Pessoa   333
A Theory of Reading   334
Concerto Piccolo   335
Eisenstadt   336
The Painting Stick   337
Rag-a-Bone   340

Venetian Castle: Iraklion 342
Knossos 344
Arkadi 345
Pan 346
Antiquities 347
Airports 348
Elysium Britannicum 350
On the Train to Shoreham 351
Near Porthcothan 352

XXI

A Short Narrative of the Restauration of His Majesty,
    by John Aubrey, Esq., F.R.S. 354

SEVEN (2008–2012)

XXII

The Poetry of Place 366
The Cornish Hedge 369
August Lines 374
At Hase-dera 380

XXIII

A Letter from Ishinomaki 382
An Unseen Crow 384

XXIV

Listening to Jazz All Day 386
Weathering 387
Reading Philip Whalen 388

Watching Birds Eat   389
Remembering Lol Coxhill   390
Listening to the Wallpaper   391
Sitting, Eating, Standing Still and Walking in Athens   392
Passing Time   394
Crossing the Thessalian Plain   395
Seeing Sights in Venice   396
Visiting the Orient   397
Travelling North from St Pancras in December   398
Being in Tune   399
Recommending Tristano   400

XXV

Knowing One's Place   404
Knowing One's Place: Part 2   407
Visiting the Ancestors   408
Looking at The City from Parliament Hill   412
Dropping In On Magnus the Martyr   414
Dining Out in Kyodo Itchome   415

XXVI

Towne, Haven & Countrey Adjoyning   418
The Cornish House   424
The Invention of the Lake District   426
Words by Samuel Palmer & His Son Herbert   430
Piet Mondrian in Belsize Park   433

XXVII

Mary Celeste   438
Homage to WCW   439
Ars Poetica   440
Bonfire of the Adjectives   441
These Be The Words   442

EIGHT (2012–2019)

XXVIII

Pythagorean 446
Difference & Repetition 447
En Route 448
Sea-Change 449
Islanded 450

XXIX

North 456
Local Ingredients 459
Loquitur 467
Temple Garden 468
Temple, Workmen, Crane, Large Rock 468
Buson's Deer, Issa's Rain, Chiyo's Frog 469
Tour Guide 470
The Sandpit Trap 472
Orpheus 473
The Pleasures of Peace 474
A Visit to Runmarö 476
West 478
On the Train to Worcester 493

Notes, Sources, Thanks 496

PASSAGES

PASSAGES

corridors

roads, paths, or channels

ways of entering or exiting

movements from one place to another

transitions from one stage or condition to another

continuous movements or flow

journeys to distant places

areas of detail in a work of art

areas of repeated small uniform-sized brush strokes

brief sections of a written or musical work

ONE

(1969)

I

SEAFARER

after the Old English

I

And now I fashion a tale of my travels,
iron-hard days when my blood
beat like a hammer, and brine-bitter sorrow
drenched this rib-shackled ache of a heart.

Cold afflicted my limbs and numbed them
when, fettered by frost at boat's prow,
I spent all the eye-straining night watch
flinching near spray-flecked cliffs.

Wine-flushed, pride-flushed,
rooted among kin on the flourishing earth,
how can a landsman know of a winter
passed on the paths of the sea?

Roar of the ocean,
the slamming of waves on the hull –
and at times the call of a swan,
a gannet's cry or curlew's whistle:
these became for me the laughter and song
of gathered kin in a fire-lit hall –
the clamour of gulls my mead.

Hail showers flew.
Storms beat on high stone cliffs.
Nesting kittiwake, icy-feathered eagle,
flung their cries on the wind.

2

The shadow of night grows dark.
Snow from the north. Grains of hail
fall on frost-gripped earth.

No haven on land for a life
blown to tatters by winter gales.

Troubled by thoughts of towering seas,
I hear the creak of tackle
as desire to set forth floods through my heart
in a welter of salt spray and tides.

3

In this valley by the shore, spring
clouds trees with blossom, scatters
a light snowfall of flowers on fields.

In the wind I hear the whisper of the sea,
and, sounding over meadows,
the cuckoo's lament,
heralding summer and singing of grief.

A gull cries as it wheels in flight
and spirit sheds land like a coat,
wings to whale-haunted seas, travels
the turning, tide-pulled world until
unquenched
it comes home to roost in my heart again.

4

Broken roofs, shattered walls, heaps
of weed-buckled masonry, stones crumbling
beneath winter's white lace of frost.
Age undermined them, grassed them over,
both buildings and builders; and others
now live by the windswept barrows,
bowed down by their dreams as they toil.

We soon turn a corner and meet
old age, look in a mirror one morning
and are ambushed by grey hair,
greying face and failing sight.

What use placing gold in a brother's grave?
No rite or observance will lighten the night
of a body that tastes neither sweetness nor pain,
stirs no limb, ponders nothing,
no thought scurrying in the empty skull.

5

A wave of the sea,
a ripple of wind in downland grasses.

Spring night, creak of tackle,
hawsers cast off from the wharf;
harbour lights flicker on water
as boat lifts prow to greet
the first wave beyond the harbour's mouth
and Orion standing tiptoe on the horizon's line.

BASHŌ

after Matsuo Bashō's Genjuan no Fu

I

Fifty years. My body, gnarled,
an old tree which bears bitter peaches;
a larva with no cocoon,
a snail without a shell.
Wind-rift, cloud-drift, knowing
no destination, morning and evening
I have eaten traveller's fare
and held out my scrip for alms.

Last year, on my journey, my face
was burnt by the sun of Matsushima.
Skin taut and sore on my cheekbones,
I longed for that farthest shore
where puffins cry and a thousand
sea-scattered islands can be seen
from the drop of a steep northern cliff.

My companion held me back. Dangers
of the journey. Sickness. Age.

Bruised heels then, stumbling in dunes
on the rough northern coast, each step
a jolt to the bone, heels crunching grit.

But then this spring I wandered
by misty lake shores, reed-fledged
water's edge, looking for a place to rest,
a single stalk of reed
where a grebe's nest might be tethered,
might be borne by the current to rest.

Bamboo, brushwood, tall grasses,
a thatched hut abandoned deep in a thicket:
the crossroads of emptiness.

World dust, crust
of cities, sifts away.

Rotting walls, damp thatch,
wrinkled bark on an ageing tree,
tang of bitter fruit.

River-run, swift
        on sand. Rinse, sift
                by reeds, water's drift.

2

Few houses here where I have my hut –

a fragrant south wind from the heights,
a north wind cool from the distant sea.

It was early summer when I came here,
azaleas blooming, and mountain wisteria
hung from the pines. Cuckoos,
swallows' visits, the glance of wings …

Silence.
Tap of a woodpecker's beak on wood.

I called out to the wood dove:

> *Come, bird of solitude,*
> *can't you provide a plaintive note?*

It was impossible not to be happy.

3

Clouded mountains, the pine of Karasaki,
wisps of mist, at times
a castle glimpsed amongst trees.
By the bridge over the shallow river
the hush and lisp of rain
quietens the waves of the lake,
the farther shore buried in mist.

Rain clears: peck of single drops
on wind-puckered lake water.
Tattered clouds. Late sunset lingers
in wet and scented pine groves,
damp brown needles beneath the quiet feet.

Mount Mikami looks like Fuji,
reminds me of my old cottage at its foot;
Mount Tanagami is haunted by the verses
of the ancients whose graves are on its slopes.

From time to time
I climb the peak behind my hut, and spread
a round straw mat on a pine bough shelf.

I call it my 'monkey's perch' –
and would never change it
for Hsü Ch'üan's drunken nest up a crab apple tree,
nor for the hermit's hut
strung together by Wang the Sage.

I sit on the summit,
picking and crushing lice.

4

Now and then
I set out to gather firewood – dry
branches in awkward bundles,
a small man in a baggy half coat
moving among the pines –

or draw spring water:

        clear drops
        trickle along the green
        of a single spray of fern.

Nothing weighs less than my stove.

5

A household shrine, an alcove
for hanging night clothes,
no other clutter from the man
who once lived here – just a plaque
with two words in a flowing hand:

Illusory
Dwelling

The calligrapher signed his name on the back –
a memento for those who might see it.

6

A passing traveller. My rush raincoat,
my broad-brimmed hat of nettle wood,
hang on a post above my pillow.

Daytime, and people come –

    villagers from the foot of the mountain
        (boars are grubbing the rice seedlings)
    or the old man from the shrine
        (rabbits are infesting the bean fields) –

and when, rarely, an old friend
comes on a visit from the distant city,
we sit at night
with the moonlight as our companion –

    hush of pines,
        whisper of stars,
   distant waters'
        ripple and lilt –

and argue quietly with our shadows.

7

Why do I live like this? Not because
I want to be a solitary in the wilderness
obliterating all my traces
with handfuls of dust. Rather, let's say
I'm an old man, in indifferent health,
grown weary of people …

What is there to say?

All my fifty years I've been a wanderer,
a man of uncommon ways, aimless
as the wind and clouds, and never
(although I've envied them, it's true)
the married man content with cities,
the official with his grant of lands –
nor even the monk who paces out his days
within the four strict walls of the Buddha's law.

But once I discovered I could make
my eccentricities a source of livelihood
(a passing whim of the world
I thought at first), I found my course set

and myself shackled for life
to the one horizon-bound line of my art.

Labour in vain:
wrinkled bark, bitter fruit.

8

Autumn is half over now:

        wind-rift,
               cloud-drift
        morning, evening,
               river-run, swift,

        a single stalk
               of reed,
        of sedge, at
               water's edge –

is there any dwelling on earth
which is not an illusory dwelling?

The thought goes, and I go to bed.

TWO

(1969–1981)

II

An autumn evening in the garden.
Moon rising, birds in their nests,
I sit among trees, alone.

Good now to play this white wood lute …
I lay the book aside and watch
the moon begin its climb behind the trees.

The distant clatter of a commuter train,
a police siren Dopplering and diminishing,
the ceaseless weave of traffic in Shibuya –

a faint rim of sound
around the outer edge of nightfall.
Meanwhile, not so far from here,

automatic weapons in their hands
and Hendrix pulsing in their heads,
young draftees head back to base.

Burnt villages, corpses in paddy fields,
refugees – the T'ang poets had seen all that.
A sleepy chirp from deep

within the bamboo thicket.
Lute sounds linger, fading, cease –
autumn night, dark – that trembling leaf …

CLUB MUGEN

Heading into town.
Slick wet tarmac on a rainy night –
a blast of neon and the taxi skids.

So then I sit at the bar and drink
while music throbs and liquid lights
blink and blob and flash.

Sexy Suzy spots me,
sashays across the dance floor
and sits herself beside me, laughing.

He thought, she says, *that he was being big-time!*
Five thousand yen?
I don't take even my eyelashes off for that!

By the Gents
a GI borrows money from his buddies
then crosses the floor towards us.

You laughin' at me, kid?

It's Joe Self, shamed and baring teeth,
that makes this scene I see,
assigns the parts we play.

Nothing to laugh about here, I say.

Tokyo, 1969

ANGKOR

I am a stone temple sunk in the green deep-water light of the
jungle. Carved gods, goddesses, kings, queens, maidens and
armies: the friezes sing on my skin.

Tree roots probe and prise my body apart, the slow violence
of the centuries stone by stone displacing and tearing down
all the works of man – until I am inhabited by landscape.

Now I know how it is for the elephant and the gnat, for
the water turning the squeaking irrigation wheels, for the
muddy fields that soak the water up, for the wind and trees
and stones and snakes, and for the monkeys who lope and
quarrel through the upper branches in sunlight.

I am a clot of leaf mould on the jungle floor, dreaming of a
splintered goddess carved in dancing stone.

Siem Reap, 1970

JANTAR MANTAR OBSERVATORY

Axis of the earth, equator's line,
phases of the moon, time all round the turning globe –
an eighteenth-century de Chirico
built them here in brick and stone.

Calendars and calculators,
planes and curves in salmon-coloured brick,
fluted pillars, a small coliseum,
a pink stuccoed staircase going nowhere –

a surrealist's village square, set down
among palm trees and parched grass
where children scamper
and young men lounge in groups and laugh.

A hot night; swirls of blossom;
dry leaves crackle under my feet as I walk.
The constellations are racing away from us
in a kalpa-long explosion,

but the sky above Jai Singh's garden of astronomy
moves without fault.
The planet spins in space.
The stars sail heaven on their perfect courses.

New Delhi, 1970

BARE ROCK

I

Poured out in lava, or bedded down
grain by filtering grain in prehistoric seas,

pressured, shifted sideways
by the planet's wrinkling crust,

scratched and scraped by glaciers,
worn smooth by water, split by frost:

time itself in the waver of its grain,
in its rough and smooth, its hard and soft.

2

Crossing a pass in late afternoon light,
pitching a small tent at sunset,

busy with guy ropes and sleeping bags
among slabs, boulders and scree;

as the light fails we heat water
over a bud of hissing blue flame,

and sit at ease, leaning our backs against
five hundred million years of stone.

Cumbria, 1973

ALPINE

1

mountain silence

boulders, sunlit scree
feet picking their own way through

2

stony summit

one blue flower in a cranny

a petal of sky

3

a gap in the cloud
blue tarn

a thousand lonely feet below

CLIMBING ROCK

> *it is thought that beyond this point*
> *it would be impossible to retreat*
> (Climbing guidebook)

1

Move up, peer round – the rope
snakes down through space behind.

All the complicated act
of strength and human balance
just keeps you here, toes
lodged on half-inch ledges, fingertips
probing rock for cracks and faults
and little incut holds

so rock can let you past.

2

Watching rock: an art.

Sometimes it seems to breathe –
holds grow bigger as you gaze,
diminish when seen through fear.

Keep looking until you see the way.

3

Step left on little flakes, reach around
to find the hidden hold – an awkward step –
bridge out across the groove –

your life depends
(the crux just up ahead)

on gravity, which keeps you here
but will kill you if you fall.

4

Legs stretched to their limits,
fingers wrestling with the crack,
one good handhold, but beyond my reach,
there's no way out or off –

I *must* go up!

One small pinch grip
and a sloping pressure hold
is what I have to get me there:

> feet higher, friction on sheer rock,
> arms and legs
> trembling from the strain –

got it!
pull up, quickly jam that crack –

made it – up and over,
high and trembling on a ledge.

5

Belay to a spike,
take in the rope, see again
cloud shadows and sunlight flow
over crags and scree.

The rope snakes down through space.
Two more pitches yet.

Climbing!

A shout floats up from below
as your second begins
to make his move

up towards the Move.

USES OF THE SEASHORE

1

Lark's twitter, rise and fall;
lapwings tumble in the air;
slow, in creeks, all day,
shelduck feed in pairs.

2

Slender wings, forked tails,
terns fly dancing out to sea to dive
for little silver wriggling fish
caught in small sharp beaks.

3

Glittering sunlight, distant sea;
a stiff-legged flock
of dunlins probes the low-tide sand flats –

        all take off at once –

a cloud of wings
that veers above the water's edge
then spirals down to feed again.

4

Sitting cross-legged in the dunes
by a wind-blown driftwood fire.
Sunset fades to starlight. The tide scrolls in,
printing tomorrow's script of ripples on the sand.

III

a drawing of attention : *a paring down*
a glacier's leavings : *a standing stone*
a message from a frontier : *a song from outside four walls*
an unpredicted naming : *a greening tree*

a cat among the pigeons
polemics
literature put to rights
green eyes, sharp red pointed beard –
knew Kensington stone by stone

Piazza San Marco,
white-haired among the pigeons

> *it isn't so, not strictly so,*
> *that's the trouble …*

that I lost my centre fighting the world …

> *– You ordered this for me?*
> *– Yes, Ezra, eat it.*

tempus tacendi, let the light speak

a bone-white sky
pale brown and yellow marsh grass
a cold wind ruffles the reed beds at Torcello

VISITING WEI PA AFTER TWENTY YEARS

after Tu Fu

fresh-cut green spring chives
        still wet from the rainy darkness,
fresh boiled rice and yellow millet

        each night
        Scorpio rises as Orion sets

but tonight we've slipped past fate
and sit sharing the light of this lamp

you fill my cup again and again

        'we don't meet so often …'

half our friends are dead,
their ghosts cry out in our hearts

        twenty years
        a friendship lasting twenty years

tomorrow
the mountains will be between us

once again
travelling different paths

MAD SONG

I gave my wits away:
they made a rotten staff.
In the dark wood, in the thicket,
I dance a tangled dance.

They came, they watched,
they asked me who I was.

I am dream, I said –
cloudless mirror, star-filled sky;
I gaze all night and never wink,
the full moon is my eye.

And I am weather, I topple trees
and beat the harvest flat;
the rain's my flail,
a hurricane under my hat.

Hold him down, they said,
put chains and bars behind those eyes.

In the dark wood, in the thicket,
I hear my tangled cry;
I gnaw my nothing to the bone,
and munch my mumble pie.

THE POEM, ALMOST

speechless, points
at the world
of which it is a part

        and which masters it
        with strangeness

and it is reduced to
penury
by the shock of that encounter

        the trees are huge
        damp living creatures

the river rushes
between its banks from all its sources

VERNACULAR

from generation to generation
passed from voice to voice
shaped and reshaped in the vortex of the throat

        cascades
        swirls and eddies

a course of rapids
a narrow gorge choked with boulders

a hanging green branch caught by flood water
vibrating in the current

        the river cuts its course

go upstream now

        drink
        from your leaky cup

cold starlight at the crystal source

ON TREVOSE HEAD

He stoops in sunlight
      patterning pebbles
brought up from the beach in a sack

a day off, and he's making
      a mosaic compass
on a high flat place by the lighthouse

Above a sea
      ruffled to points of white
by a steady south-west wind

and under an azure sky
      – a high pure lens of air –
he sets small coloured stones in place

      great-grandfather
      who I never knew

the weight of seventy years of sky
rests
on crumbling concrete and dislodged pebbles

IN THE MOUNTAINS: FOUR POEMS

November

days are short and cold
mountains turn gaunt and bare
the moon shifts through its quarters in the frosty sky

    the tide of darkness floods
    down from the pole towards December

the tarn will freeze from shore to shore

    an eyelid blinks

clear moonlight on a snowy hill

Empty House

ice crystals on sheep's droppings
hoar frost on roadside grasses

a snowflake melts on the tongue
boots squeak on frozen earth

the drystone wall
    whistles through its lichened teeth
white fell tops ache in a clear blue sky

    six senses
    a sword of ice

an empty house beneath the wind

It All Becomes Clear Sky

one day
we just lock up and leave

slates and rafters fall
    in windy attics

broken garden gate
green grass along the path

    bodies disperse
    to moorland earth

a wisp of cloud in a high northern wind

Entering

standing under
the fringe of the last pine

beyond
the last gate

in the steep
valley loud with its beck

the path leading
off through bracken

to mountains
beyond mountains

IN THE MOUNTAINS: FIVE DAYS

1

teeth chatter in the freezing dawn
hoar frost
on boulders around my sleeping bag

morning star
suspended in the brightening sky

sunlight, starlight
the huge wheel of days

2

crags
mountain grass
miles of empty sky and stone

a sheep startles –
          I watch me pass
through wary yellow eyes:

cloud of unknowing
bound up in hoof and horn,
sinew, bone and fleece

3

white sky:
a raven's call
scores a single charcoal mark upon emptiness

millennia erode into silence

clink of a
sudden small landslip

skitter of stones
dislodged from a scree slope

4

midday
doze on warm stones by a tarn

small waves scurry and splash

> *I am stone*
> *I am empty silent mountain air*

who invented the wind?

5

coming down to the valley
once again

all those miles of sky and stone

five days
hidden somewhere back up there
between the mountains and the sky

> empty places
> barren places

inexhaustibly fertile

WYTHBURN VALLEY

1

moraine
          blue sky
the valley is an empty trench
a groove of absent stone

2

pipit's whistle –
flick of a tail by a hummock of moor grass

by the tumbling beck
bird bones half-bedded in peat

we gather white branches to make our fire

3

the sky aches in its sleeve
          of earth and grass and stone
the beck rings upon emptiness

the valley dreams a cold north wind
          to feed the memory in its bones
of the absence of its maker

          a chisel of ice betrayed by climate

gravel dumped off its snout in heaps
          as it melted back towards its seed –
a single snowflake a million years before

4

we coax flame from ashes
the next grey misty morning
and then move on

small travellers
under a cloudy sky
walking the ghost of a glacier

MUSICA UNIVERSALIS

we have   the spheres   the stars

an ear   ringing   singing

which can hear   in the frosty air the winter of space

WINTERING

east wind –
on the sea wall a hundred gulls
face into it

*

rusty plough –
red hens
scratch in the farmyard

*

dry white grass stalks
rattling –
dark moorland skyline

*

frost all day
the birds
look twice as big

*

January 1st
leafless branches
last year's snow

HEBRIDEAN

tang of drifting peat smoke
gritty touch of sun-warmed granite

I sit
my back against the farmhouse wall
drinking hot sweet tea
and looking out across the sound to Jura

a snipe
        slowly builds
                its huge high tower of air
in a wind like thought itself

then spreads
vibrating tail feathers on the down-swoop

        drumming –
        isn't that what you call it?

the thrum of feathers in
the wind from off the kyle

a wind whose name is being here

Colonsay, 1977

GULF STREAM

a northern island
a sheltered valley
an untended garden

the grass-grown bed
of an empty
ornamental lake

mossy gravel path
wild rhododendrons, azaleas
a blaze of flowers

dark thick foliage
the air is heavy with scent
hidden birds call

a microclimate
a message
whispered across an ocean

the sea
which can bring such tidings
five thousand miles

Colonsay, 1977

CROSSING THE PASS

snow patches
                a cairn
a prayer flag
fluent on its bending pole
a clear high wind from the uplands

crossing the pass
        everything is air and light –
new territory, the first look in
to an unknown land

                high plateau
                the roof of the mind

it is neither the flag nor the wind
it is your mind that flaps

the ceiling of the world flows
slowly overhead

     barred fish-scale clouds
     like wave ripples traced on sand

the river rushes towards the sea
wind floods through the trees
the ruined castle stone by stone
pours itself back into earth

     full moon
     ave regina cœlorum

twenty miles from here
at your behest, beneath your light
the tide sheets in like clouds
across miles of sandflats, Morecambe Bay

my head is a high bald hill
the palm of my hand a moonlit beach

     fingerprints
     whorls and creases
     lines written on the palm

tide patterns wrinkled in the sand

Kendal, 1978

THE GATE

He came a long way round
by steep paths through tangled mountains,
and when at last he came

to the appointed place, he nearly failed
to know it, except that the sunlit path looked
so right for just a moment.

Here he found the riddle of his heart deciphered,
its geography laid out before his eyes
like paradise seen from a hilltop;

here he saw his griefs
like wisps of smoke from distant chimneys
dissolving in the placid air;

and, just as his forgotten dream had foretold,
the gate swung open at the sound
of his footfall, admitting him to

a landscape loud with birds, which sang
to tell him that the regime had fallen,
that the lair of power was destroyed for ever.

IV

HEARING THE BLACK-THROATED DIVERS CALL

I

marsh gentian
cross-leaved heath (or: *bog heather*)
tufted vetch (fern-like leaves, dangling purple bells)
bog asphodel (a spike of yellow stars)
lousewort
        (clustered pinkish-purple flowers and wrinkled leaves)
delicate, delicate harebells
birdsfoot trefoil (yellow gorse-like clusters –
        bacon and egg, lady's finger, lady's slipper,
        fingers and thumbs, Tom Thumb)
tormentil (yellow, four petals, deep-toothed leaves –
        'the roots boiled in milk are efficacious for diarrhoea')
eyebright (small and white)

2

six ravens
a pair of peregrine falcons (with young)

a heronry in the pine trees at the water's edge
        (three nests though one seems deserted)
the adults sit with dignity in the tree tops
come and go with lazy wing flaps and trailing legs

the racket of the chicks being fed
squalls across the quiet waters of the loch

3

dawn
still water
standing reeds
a trout jumps and plops
the distant bulk of Ben Nevis blue in early morning light

mid-morning
chaffinches chirple
black-throated divers dive
a foraging treecreeper spirals up a tree trunk
a goldcrest among dark spruce whittles away at the silence

4

Lochan a' Ghiubhais   : small loch of the fir tree
Lochan nam Breac   : small loch of the trout
Lochan an Eisg Mor   : small loch of the big fish
Lochan Edin   : small loch of the birds
Lochan na h-Aon Chraoibh : small loch of the single tree

5

at Beallach Dubh
                (black pass)
boot soles whisper to dark earth
in windless peat-hag corridors –

        hushed maze-like passages
        between fibrous walls
                crowned with sphagnum moss,
        heather, grass and sedges –

then out!
green mountains
        episodic sun and cloud
a contoured path descending
to an abandoned croft beside a lochan

swim
in cold (with sudden warm patches) peaty water –
wavering limbs a radiant orange-brown

        wagtails bob and dip
                on lochside boulders
        a solitary immature gull
                sits on a rock in the burn

6

return to the hostel by evening
        weather sweeping in
the surface of the loch
        roiled to confusion
        by veering and backing gusts –
dark sky, downpour, thunderclaps –
lightning makes everything as clear as day

the storm passes into the neighbouring glen
        where it roars and flashes
                distantly and more distantly
until midnight
when I go back outside
and hear the black-throated divers calling in the dark

Loch Ossian, 4–9 August 1975

LOOKING AT THE WORK KEN WALL DOES

a curated bookcase

top shelf:	model hippopotamus four peanuts

2nd shelf: Coke bottle painted gold
small box containing lead weight on piece of string

3rd shelf: box containing fossil Mesozoic-era snail (225–265 million years ago), shell of modern garden snail, and card explaining that snails live for 4–5 years and are hermaphrodite

4th shelf: one raisin
sewing kit

bottom shelf: a rack of rusty nails

I tried to work in a factory and in an office
now this is the work I do

a trouser-shaped piece of grey canvas with a breech-flap

eight snail shells glued to the wall in a vee – a flight of wild gasteropods

a pickled bat in a square glass jar

a hank of sheep's wool threaded through a towel ring

a hangman's noose

a cobbler's last dangling on a rope

if you step outside Western 'reality',
the nose-to-the-grindstone materialism and rat-race, then
the incident becomes dominant

Two riding-boot stretchers laid on the floor; a pair of rusty iron balls
between them, connected by rope to an abdominal mirror adorned
with intestinal coiled brass tubing; a wood-framed X-ray of a rib cage
sits up at an angle of 45 degrees; above this, a wooden box suspended
from the ceiling contains a plaster of Paris head with a large brass
bolt screwed firmly into its forehead.

one thing
ten thousand things
IF UNDELIVERED PLEASE RETURN TO THE BURSAR

step outside

the trees are
very bare
at this time
of year

Newcastle, 30 November 1976

I

snow falling all night –
woken twice by
        muffled thumps
as it slid off branches onto the roof

mid-morning
        big soft flakes
float and dither and drift

in the top field, sheep, fleeces
        transformed to weighty tasselled skirts
by the lumps of whiteness matted into them –
each animal hesitant, but all
behaving without hesitation as a group

        roll a large
        (larger and larger) snowball down the slope
        to bare some grass for them to eat

the snow stops
the sun breaks through

the long white ridge of the High Street range
traversed by the Roman road
                from Brocavum to Galava
        (thereafter a peat cutters' packhorse track
        and site of summer fairs –
wrestling, horse racing, lost sheep returned to their owners)

shines out against a troubled sky

2

clear sky today

walk in sunshine down Correction Hill
to the town in its hollow, where settled snow
highlights limestone planes and angles

     how to make a picture – abstract
     or semi-abstract – to capture
     the shapes, the colour values of this

so a Kendalian seeing it anywhere might think
that calls Kendal to mind –
          the town evoked
by a nearly cubist configuration
of grey, interlocking, roof-shaped planes
set down – just so – below a complex angled line:

the snowy ridge of the High Street range
sharp now
against a blue winter sky

Kendal, 31 January–1 February 1977

HITCHHIKING TO CORNWALL, PAYING TWO VISITS, AND HITCHHIKING BACK AGAIN

I

cloudy, warm,
spatters of rain, but clearing later

    wooded richness west of Exeter

a Land Rover, driven by (*what!*) Mick Taylor
now getting his post-Stones band together

    we've toured Britain and Europe
    but in the autumn we're doing the States –
    that has to be the one

why the Land Rover?

    because it's fun
    because no one argues with it in London
    and because the cottage on Dartmoor's two miles from the road

9 p.m., a roundabout outside Plymouth:
liquid stars
suspended in a dove-grey sky

to Bodmin
with a Londoner working at Wheal Jane

    tin, copper, silver (plus, in the old days, arsenic,
    sulphur, tungsten, zinc, iron, and ochre)
    government subsidies just to keep the pumps at work

he and his wife gave notice on the flat in Brixton
sold the furniture
put the kids in the back of the car
and drove to Cornwall with £250

it worked out all right, but
it could just as easily have gone the other way –
scares me to death when I think about it now

2

with Eileen to Bodmin to visit Grandpa
(who saw the poppies bloom
                    in no man's land, 1917)
gaunt and frail, helped by a nurse
to where we wait in the visitors' room

    – how's your chest now, Edwin?
    – oh, fine, goat's milk, you know
    – goat's milk?
    – yes, where do you get yours from?

he says he's gone deaf
yet can hear Eileen but not me
    (although he recognises me well enough)

difficult silences
we watch him turn things over in his head

in the end he shrugs and asks us to leave

3

visit Gladys in Rock:
how it was when Grandpa went off his head

    his delusions
    her secret phone call to the doctor

he tried to leg it
but the ambulance was blocking the gate
they cornered him by the garage, straitjacketed him
and carried him kicking away

4

grey dawn
tamarisk trees, hedges, dunes, grey sea
a patter of raindrops on my cagoule hood

later: sunshine, grained sand
sea-smoothed pebbles at the tideline
the folded strata of the cliffs

gulls lift off the beach with a little run
and fly out low over incoming waves

5

leave at 7 a.m.
Plymouth to Exeter, an ex-Warrant Officer
(twenty-two years in Coastal Command)

Shackletons:

> *forty thousand rivets in loose formation*
> *spilling oil all over the world*

he quit because of Nimrod:
        flying jets was too professional,
technology destroyed
the *esprit de corps* that made it all worthwhile

I remember once
we walked down from the base in Singapore
and looked in a tailor shop window;
the Chinese owner came out and said

> *— you are aircrew*
> *— yes, how did you know?*
> *— ground crew always come alone, aircrew together*

dead true, although I'd never noticed it myself
and I pride myself on being observant

a market gardener now and keeps a few pigs

6

leaving Exeter
a businessman in a Cortina
picks up a young marine and gets me too

nineteen years old
fed up with the service

> *45 Commando is jungle-trained,*
> *41 is snow-trained,*
> *but all we're good for is digging trenches on Dartmoor*

he'd been in Ulster and had shot a dog –
    with his mates had had a laugh
when a Catholic who gave them lip
was made to stand in the rain while they took his car to bits

the driver drops him off near Teignmouth

> *hard as nails, that boy,*
> *hard as nails, he'd smile while he killed you,*
> *they're quite superb – I know a lot of those lads –*
> *and technically so good*

7

eleven hours at Gordano Services

> so boring, so frustrating
> that in the end it becomes interesting again

an ex-India traveller, an ex-squaddie,
      a youth worker from Moss Side
a roundabout, a roadside, cups of tea in the café
hours
with thumb raised to the stream of traffic

> and then
> at last
> at 11 p.m.

a lift from two Scousers in a Transit
all the way to Knutsford

A38, Bodmin, Rock, Trevone, A38, M5, 14–18 May 1978

V

SEEING SIGHTS IN SANCTUARY WOOD

Hill 62, Ypres Salient

1

tree stumps
          pockmarked
by the bullets of sixty years ago

               shattered rifles
                         among new leaves and saplings
               split-open gas canisters, a derelict mortar
               deep-dented helmets, rust-flaked shell cases

the muddy-bottomed trench
five feet deep, firing step supported by
          corroded sheets of corrugated iron
zigzags for fifty yards to the border of the wood

beyond the fence, a field
ploughed level, green with corn

               a tractor working,
               its distant grumble
               filtering through April birdsong

2

on tables inside the museum
small polished wooden boxes
eyeholes on the front and a handle on the side
sepia 3-D photographs, thirty or forty to a box

               turn the handle
               raise up an image before your eyes

five soldiers sit in a shell-hole having a smoke
two soldiers, tunics open, boots off
          share a loaf of bread in the sun
a single soldier treads a greasy duckboard
          through the oceanic mud of Passchendaele

eyes of shell-shocked men
stare out at us and into a far dark distance
as they stared sixty years ago
through and beyond the man with the camera

legless, armless, headless corpses in mud
bones protruding through
          blackened flesh or tattered cloth
a skeletal hand still grips a rifle
a skull's top half lies
          two feet from its jaw and cheekbones

> *Soldiers of the Great War*
> *Known Unto God*

the souvenir shop offers
guidebooks, postcards, mugs, statuettes, plaques,
polished brass cartridges
and ashtrays made from sawn-off shell cases

THE TEMPTATION OF ST ANTHONY

Hieronymus Bosch

this one has a pig snout and cunning eyes
he holds out his cup for wine
an owl is perched on his head

this one wears a bishop's robes
blood pours from his back
he disputes a sacred text with a bird and a fish

this one is obsequious
he carries a frog on a silver platter
the frog also carries a platter

this one is serious
he wears a tall black hat
a blackbird's claw sticks out from under his cloak

this one has no arms
he is up to his waist in water
a bowl of porridge is balanced on his head

this one is naked
he blows a trumpet
a sausage pops out on a string

and here is a pig
an earthen pitcher
which pisses from its bunghole

and here is Mr Burgher
with his missus
riding complacently through the sky on a fish

over here is a burning town
and these are the winged devils
who wheel among the flames

over there is a marching army
this here is a gibbet
and these are human bones scattered on the ground

but who is this
cloaked and bearded figure
the still point at the hub of this demented mandala?

just one more figure in a sea of hallucination
but the only one who looks us in the eye
mon semblable, mon frère, he stares straight out at us

his eyes are haunted
unexpectant
with just a trace of mockery

and even though he
long ago finished with questions

his eyes ask

do you also see truly
are you also a witness?

THREE

(1978–1981)

VI

THE DANCER AND THE DANCE

Elizabeth Walton at the Riverside Studios

Part 1: *Preparation*

a woman in a leotard
arranges her props and speaks a word:

 performance

and then another word:

 preparation

she makes a repeated awkward movement
on a dais at the back of the stage

to do this over and over again, she says
until it's just right

I have, she says, *to have you watch this
even though it scares me*

is it all right, she asks
to spend your life preparing for something that has no purpose?

Part 2: *Technique*

she hangs a six-foot sheet of paper
on the wall at the back of the stage

in front of it she does the dance of dancing
the dance of technique
a torrent of asanas cascading one into another
balletic runs broken by virtuoso leaps and floatings

she launches herself again and again into air
at each gravity-free juncture
she flashes us a switched-on smile

with a felt tip marker on the sheet she draws
the stylised figure of a dancer
she stands in front of it
in the posture of Vitruvian man

a trembling begins at the tips of her fingers
spreads down her arms, engulfs her body
and throws her to the floor in spasm

she leaps to her feet
tears down the paper and crumples it

Part 3: *Dance*

a tape of fragmented sounds
of silences
of city noises
a soundtrack to which she starts to move, austerely

the sounds don't say anything
or lead anywhere
or add up to anything
they're simply there

keeping such company her body is simply there
her movements occur
in a space opened by the soundtrack
in which she encounters and counterpoints the sounds

the dance has become its own language
no longer to be spoken of
it speaks
she calls it *A New Life*

ATTENTION

the railway workers
cross the line
stepping

casually
over one
live rail

(turning to
each other
and talking)

and then
the other – they
do this every

day, almost
not noticing
they're doing it

carefully

NIGHTCLUB WORK

She steps onto the dance floor
and turns with a beautiful

practised gesture, seasoned with
a brittle nostalgia for

how it was meant to have been:
a teenage girl's winning ways

blossoming into a bride's
unblemished expectancy.

Whose dream was it anyway,
and who is it really for,

this spell she casts on the air
with only the curve of her

body to assist her? He
leaves the men at the table,

takes hold of her, clumsily,
in his excitement, in his

drunkenness, and together
they dance on the darkened floor.

MARKET

close-set scales
        doleful mouths, insensate eyes
thousands
shining silver bodies in orange wooden boxes

        (early morning light
        concrete quayside, Aberdeen)

whole shoals lifted late last night
in squirming, dripping sacks
        out of the cold North Sea
to drown in air

longliners
            purse seiners
                        factory trawlers

somewhere soon the world's last
        cold-blooded aquatic vertebrate
is hiding in a hole at the bottom of the sea

            fish eye
            fish bone

            fish finger

unlike us
they mostly have no eyelids

COVENT COMMUNITY GARDEN

a green place deep in a socket
where a building has been pulled like a tooth

where earth, brought in by truckloads,
is cared for under this sign:

TO BE REDEVELOPED:
300,000 SQUARE FEET
OF OFFICE SPACE

lumpy squares
      of threadbare turf,
tulips, pansies and forget-me-nots

a bee buzzes in an acoustic foxglove
beside a stack of ruined brickwork .

a thrush sings beneath grey skies

a tranquillity
a made space among
      the shifting concrete pack-ice slabs
of property and finance

*'we work in the garden
as if it was going to be here forever –*

    there is no other way'

CRYSTAL

for Ursula

you showed me in the London street –
    among pneumatic drills,
    torn-up tarmac, traffic cones –
the crystal dangling from your key ring
preserver of sanity, you said

blue   yellow   purple   green

and suddenly a memory:

    the long lonely glen
    the great silence

blue sky over dreaming mountains
    tough grass and knotted heather
peat-stained water tumbling
down a shallow staircase of uneven stone

    deer graze high on Ben Alder's shoulder
    an eagle soars and glides

green mountains, purple heather
blue sky, yellow glinting water

    crystalline
    intersecting planes of light

a green glen
    preserver of sanity
carried
through a world of broken paving stones

99

BIRDS OF A FEATHER

1

shoveller   tufted duck   pochard   widgeon   coot

    flute and dabble in the lake

on the web-printed bank
a mallard stands with dignity on one leg

a moorhen steps meticulously over grass blades

2

the biography of a feather:

genetic fermentation in an albumen enclosure
a cracking open to light and air
down grows sleek on a plump and muscled body
a quill works loose from its socket
a shedding
a wind-quickened floating amongst shivering wavelets

soon to be mulch
soon to be less than that

3

the rotund goose
steps down the sloping bank
on its big orange feet

then topples forward to
breast the wetness, launching itself

    into the spreading ripples of
    this glimpse, this moment of entering

the wetly sensuous world of the water
the impermeable gooseness of the goose

W. S. 1611

each word
a pebble seen through water

talismanic
        the isle is full of noises
liquid clarity of hallucination

'characters'
            the machinery of the stage
he works like a carpenter at odds with
barely adequate materials

        to fly
        to swim
        to dive into the fire
        to ride on the curled clouds

a lifetime in
the conjuror's profession

        his dreaming eye is wide open

the baseless fabric of this vision

ARIEL

active   mobile   piercing

prompt in learning or perception

the sensitive parts, esp. under the fingernails
the tenderest feelings

     quick-born
     quick-change
     quick-eyed
     quick-fire
     quick-scented
     quick-sighted
     quick-silver
     quick-witted

Old Norse   *kvikr*
Old English   *cwic*

     living

my dainty Ariel: I shall miss thee

I eat my pizza in a cave at the base of a concrete cliff
Wine glasses glow on tablecloths like votive lamps
The room brims with a hundred overlapping voices
The waiters come and go like shuttles on a weaving frame
Pizzas arrive on tables (service is not included)
Edible flowers in a tapestry of wine, white linen and bonhomie

The chef labours at his forge
Slaps out dough on his marble-topped anvil
Stokes the furnace which drives this merry-go-round
This Catherine wheel
This warped rock 'n' roll revolving in the cave of a neon-lit jukebox

It's warm tonight
But the air conditioner is an open doorway
Feeding us a stream of Arctic tundra prehistoric air

And suddenly I find myself transported
To a chilly place of huge horizons
I look around, I'm surprised to be here
But not more surprised than anyone else
The chef, the waiters, the pizza-eaters interrupted in mid-mouthful
All clothed now in sheepskins and snug leather caps with woollen earflaps
And seated astride lean fierce horses with twitching flanks

But we get used to it
Our exclamations dissolve in the frosty air
We fall silent, we grow expectant, we begin to understand
We've been assembled here for something momentous
Something that will declare itself in this frozen space
Where pools of blood in the snow look like flowers
Look much like pizzas on a tundra-sized tablecloth

We wait
We listen to the wind
We've edged our knives and whetted our wits
We've honed our hunger to an asceticism so sharp
That we can chop down skyscrapers just by thinking about it
At any moment now we'll sweep down
To take our places at the tables we reserved
By planting a seed in a telephone five thousand years ago

And at that moment
Every telephone in the world will ring
And a strangely familiar voice will announce
In a language no one has heard before but anyone can understand
That a cast of billions has been assembled, that now we can bring you
At great expense and all the way from nowhere
The greatest show on earth, it will last for one-tenth of a second

LES SALTIMBANQUES DE WESTBOURNE PARK

hommage à Guillaume Apollinaire

I cycle uphill in the dark
Below the tower block, a searchlight in its forehead
Past the construction site grinding its teeth under floodlights
Under the belly of the concrete motorway centipede

Then up to the crest of the hill
And the iron bridge over the old canal
A placid curve of water singing
Forgotten nineteenth-century songs under its damp and misty breath

Tonight a crowd has assembled on the bridge
Others have gathered on the towpath below
As I arrive there's an explosion –
A bomb! is it a bomb? no, it's a firework

We peer across the water to
A commotion being enacted in a derelict back garden
Mysterious figures by torchlight
Trying to lift a large black ball out of the water

Oh, it's a what-d'you-call-it, a community festival
Torches burn, the water runs gold, red and black
The crowd are like bees trying to remember
Something they once knew about flowers

A van with dented panels swerves to a halt by the curb
Two Black youths jump out of it
One wears stone-washed jeans and T-shirt taut over bulging muscles
The other, shades and a floppy hat at the hippest possible angle

A police car crawls towards us and gives us all a stare
Probes for misdemeanours with its headlights
Radio crackles, tyres squeal, blue lights flash
The siren fades from earshot, life goes on

A loudspeaker clears its throat and a voice announces
That Thanks to Our Patient Participation in Today's Events
The End of the World
Has Been Postponed for a Few More Weeks

The voice is tired
Tired with being an underpaid social policy graduate in 1979
Tired with the friction between the word *patient*
And the word *participation*

A smattering of applause
A small shower on a summer night
Uncertain celebrations
City of rotten molars

cycling along Great Western Road on my way to Fulham
I pass a woman in bright sari and multicoloured choli
waiting for a bus by a scaffolded building
and suddenly I'm back in Calcutta

      coriander, cow-dung, charcoal smoke
      dust stained red with squirts of betel juice,
      drinking hot sweet tea
      from a small cup made of earth

well, I wish I was in West Bengal, but here I am
cycling now along the North End Road

      home appliance outlets, wet fish shops
      bookmakers, discount clothing stores
      the street market in full vociferous cry
      squshd vgtbls in the gutters

I chain the bike to a lamp post
go into the new flat to get the electricity connected
the task completed by an ageing actor
who does this kind of thing when he's resting

      terrible, dear, thank you for asking,
      I've just broken my top set –
      and my first recording for months to do tonight –
      yes, that's right – sw6, *spelt* T-H-I-X

spare keys from the landlord in his butcher's shop
ruddy-faced emperor of a white-tiled pandemonium

      blood-stained aprons, shouts of the lads
      whack of cleavers on chopping blocks
      huge sides of beef sway on stainless steel hooks

but even the stink of blood doesn't dismay me today
life is good, and anything is welcome to a place in this poem

across the street a Polo Mint ad on a hoarding tells me:

nothing is a patch on a hole in your pocket

ABOUT A MARRIAGE

for Jane

a Sunday drive
just the two of them
she driving
he beside her reading the map

his intense fragility, she thought, *his distance*

nothing to say to each other now without the kids
as they drove through mist
to a place where
had there been no mist

they could have seen half the hills of England

FUNERAL

what exactly was inside that box
heaped with flowers

impossible
it should have been a person

and I had never known such absence

yet could not think of
his body as an it

no way to speak
or treat with such precision
of nothingness

ceremony without consolation
grey skies
the yew trees guttering in the wind

SEEING KUNG-SUN'S PUPIL DANCE

On 15 November 767 I saw Li-shih-er-niang dance at the house of Yuan Ch'ih, Lieutenant-Governor of K'uei province. She so impressed me that I asked her who she'd trained under, and she told me she'd been Kung-sun's pupil.

I remember seeing Kung-sun dance at Yen-ch'eng fifty years ago, when I was only a boy. The purity of her style and her incisive attack were unrivalled – no one during the early part of the Emperor's reign, before the Disturbances, understood dance as she did. Her face like jade, her brocade dress ... but I'm white-haired now, and even her pupil is past her prime.

Some years ago, Zhang Xu, the master of the grass-writing style of calligraphy, often saw Kung-sun dance at Yeh-tsien. The result, which delighted him, was that he found his calligraphy greatly improved – which tells you something about the sort of person Kung-sun was.

years ago Kung-sun astonished the world
watchers gathered around
like range beyond range of bewildered hills
and when she left the stage
heaven and earth danced on and on

she was nine suns falling out of the sky
she was dragons soaring through space
her entrance was a thunderclap
her stillness green ice and winter light

red lips
sleeves embroidered with pearls
ashes and silence

but Li-shih has caught up the fragrance
and the old mastery haunts her dance

among the Emperor's eight thousand dancers
        Kung-sun knew no equal –
fifty years turn over like the flick of a hand
dust clouds
dark winds on the palace for fifty years

the Pear Garden dancers are gone like mist
and Li-shih's face as she dances
        is like the sun in winter
saplings planted by the Emperor's tomb
have joined hands above the pathway
grass withers on the walls of set stone

the mats are edged with tortoiseshell
the urgent flutes
        fade to stillness again
at the height of pleasure comes sorrow
the moon begins its climb in the east

I am an old man
my future a tangle of mountains

my feet get weary of the path

after Tu Fu

WANG WEI WRITES A LETTER

February
clear bright weather

last night I climbed Hua-tzu Hill
a full moon on all the country
the waters of the Wang River
        rippling in its light
distant lanterns coming and going
        in cold hills beyond the woods
dogs barking in lanes
        sounding like leopards
the pounding of grain in the village
heard between strokes of a distant bell

we must wait for the spring:
green trees, green grass, green hills
steep paths beside clear streams
dace leaping out of the water
gulls soaring
dew wet on the grassy banks
the morning call of pheasants in the corn

all this will be with us soon
surely then we can go walking together?

no urgency

this comes to you by a hillman
from Wang Wei
man of the hills

A PANEL FROM THE CATHEDRAL DOOR

Hildesheim, A.D. 1015

Old Man God
            points
a wrathful finger

at the man who points
at the woman who points
at the serpent
            curled
at the foot of the tree
of all the world. What

        twist in the psyche
        brought forth dirt? The man

and the woman crouch
like strange beasts in the field
more abject than any beasts, as abject as

        some fearful adolescent
        whimpering at his prayer stool

in the field of all the world

where the goodman, the goodwoman
cringe
and try to hide their nakedness

        from that old man and his
        indignant finger –

him with The Book in his other hand.

LUNCH BREAK IN THE PARK

> *The greylag has been re-established by releasing birds in*
> *suitable areas, but the resulting flocks in southern Britain*
> *tend to be semi-tame, and to lack the special appeal of the*
> *truly wild geese to be found in Scotland.*   (RSPB)

1

the sky a jubilation of winter blue
and a wind so cold it hurts

beside the pond
a woman in a black overcoat scatters bread
to a squabble of ducks and burly geese
that seethe around her shoes and knees

an avenue of bare branches
          leads the eye to a chilly horizon
a range of office blocks
as remote and blank as an Arctic cliff

2

the pond is a circle of dazzling blue and white
with ice shards tinkling at its edges

five nodding greylags dabble and circulate
then come ashore to preen
          snaking their necks backwards
wriggling their bills in amongst their feathers –

a conclave of muscular dwarfs
in tight brown suits
meticulously checking their pockets

3

I head back towards the gate
past the silent bandstand

(wrought-iron curlicues and flutings –
a Victorian toy left out on a frosty lawn)

when suddenly:

ragged abrasive calls
extended necks and gaping orange bills
the clap of heavy wings
as a flight of greylags slams past just overhead

I walk back to my basement desk

ears ringing

with hoarse goose music and
the aftershock of wings

THE TRAMP

in the graveyard
said: Jesus

is coming soon
you know

I've only taken
to drink

as a temporary
measure

in the graveyard
said: Jesus

VII

LIMEUIL

Vézère   Dordogne
is what we called them until here

slow flow over
        rounded pebbles by the banks
deeper swifter stronger in the centre

two
greenbrown muscles of water

a high arched bridge over each of them
a green tongue of land
reaching down between them

to touch

        the unimpedable
        the unnameable

moment of meeting waters

VALLEY MORNING

1

each morning
fog curls among trees, wood smoke drifts

there should be higher ground
above these misty pine-fledged slopes

     (snowfields and naked rock
     beneath a blaze of sun)

but no, no land above 500 metres hereabouts

     we live in the foothills of
     range upon range of dreams

beaded dewdrops on the eagle's feathers

2

each wooden door is open
knock at any one you choose

mother
     father
child and grandchild
the woodman pulls on his boots

this
is the only life there is

     dog barks
     bird calls
     cock crows

first cup of coffee in the chilly dawn

HUSBANDRY

The stream tumbles down the terraced hillside
and enters the grassy, stone-walled plot
by a small fall, and then is channelled
into a rectangular pool deep enough
for the ducks and geese to swim in.

The sides of the pond are neatly fettled:
wooden stakes support caulked planks
which keep the dark earth back.
At the pool's far end, a gap in the earthen bank
is plugged with a chipped concrete block –

a lip over which the stream continues.
A cleanly incised drainage channel leads
the water along beside the boundary wall,
so the ducks and geese have not only
a pond but also enough dry ground

to feed, preen and roost on.
At the corner of the enclosure, a section
of salvaged concrete pipe directs
the water onwards. Where the stream reaches
the stony hill path, the water tumbles

over another fall and into a channel
that leads downhill towards the river.
Here, a tin can has been wedged into a cranny,
a hosepipe attached to the bottom of it.
Most of the water continues in the stream, but

the pressure drives some into the hose
and thence into the sprinkler
in the vegetable patch across the path,
where succulent aubergines glisten in sunlight
beneath a four-foot rainbow.

When not needed, remove the can from the stream.

Tursac, Dordogne, 1980

GREETINGS

In a clearing at the top of the hill
the old man is tending his vegetables,
his dog stretched out by the hedge.

He stumps back down the furrow
to greet us – *m'sieurs-et-dames* –
a strong handshake, a glint in his eye.

J'aime les Anglais, j'étais à Dunkerque,
quarante – plusieurs bombes!
He mimes the bombs and laughs at them

and at his own survival.
I ask if all three plots up here are his
and he takes me to mean, does he

own all this, as far as the eye can see?
Je suis pas capitaliste! A sweep of the hand
to the far horizon, and a huge guffaw:

Mon chien, il s'appelle Milord!

VIII

PARADEISOS

1

stone parapet
the curve of the long water

invisible shaping grammar
the human planted order
behind these self-ordered growings

various oaks
various ash and elm

paradise is not a place, but is
made and kept in mind

a tranquillity imagined
        projected onto earth
                excluding all division

the willows tremble at the water's brink

2

'garden' from Old English *geard*

fence   enclosure   dwelling

pairidaeza (Persian): walled garden
παράδεισος: enclosed garden
        orchard, pleasure ground

pairi: around
diz (Sanskrit *dih*): to mould, form, or shape
        (for example, a wall of earth)

from the Indo-European
          DHEIG: knead, mould, form
from which Latin *fingere*

figure   feign   fiction

it is planted in our tongues
the code is written in the seed

Figulus

draws the world to its lip
on the spin of his potter's wheel

3

and what is kneaded from the clay
is not the flesh

but the frontiers of our perception
a shaping grace

as now the music of this moment
this making
the shapely specificity of this world

has drawn me to the gap in the trees

          where the even turf stretches
          down to the water's edge

to drink
from this earthen cup
the fictive waters of our oldest story

ART PEPPER IN LONDON

he introduces his Bulgarian pianist as

> *a man who wanted to be free in his music*
> *so he came over here to the USA …*

London? USA?

and, then again, that word *free* …

B52s lined up on the runways
    (the free world's unsinkable aircraft carrier)
radar scanning the eastern horizon
technicians running checks in their bunkers

while in this smoky jazz club, not far from

> the threatened frontier
> the floodlit wire
> the tank tracks in the dust
> the armoured phalanxes at their war games

piano and alto sax
pour freely forth their music

> in the mode of white Los Angeles
> nineteen fifty-something

in the key of cold war minor

Ronnie Scott's, June 1980

RHYME

white plastic sandals
                hare krishna
faded orange robes
                hare krishna
grey shaven skulls
                krishna krishna
other-planet eyeballs
                hare hare

        chanting and
        ching-ching-a-ling finger-
        cymballing along
        Kensington High Street

while in a boutique behind them

        bald, ash-white and ascetic, clad
        in exquisite orange-yellow robes

a window dresser's mannequins devoutly pose

A man sits on a folding chair at a desk with a phone.
He dials. He speaks. He listens to his speaking.
He speaks a language from another planet, one
where time is different from here. No, he doesn't,
he speaks a language-like language from here
where time is no different from now. I don't
understand what he says and I don't mind a bit.

Another man steps across the wooden floor,
slow and stiff, a bit arthritic around the pelvis.
He looks out from beneath his eyebrows.
A repeated stork-like placing of the feet.
Nothing is expressed; something happens.
Someone is looking out through his eyes.

The speaking man stops speaking. Now
he's pushing a wooden chair across the floor.
The chair cries out, juddering
in the stress and tremble of its frictions.
The man allows the sounds to be, he listens,
he allows the chair to speak its say.

He pushes a blackboard, he pushes a rake,
he pushes a bright red tubular steel trolley.
Things stripped of our meanings, now at last
they can believe in themselves. No, they can't,
they're just a blackboard, a trolley, a rake, and
I've never seen such objects before. They speak.

He pushes a grand piano across the floor.
Its casters jammed, its loud pedal held down,
it squeaks and growls and grinds, the air is filled
with giddying vistas of stacked harmonics.
It sounds like the end of the world but it isn't.
What it is really is a piano being pushed
across a wooden floor. The pushing man listens.

The moving man moves. One of his hands
wriggles and flutters in front of him.
The action is tossed to the other hand
to continue. The rest of his uneventful body
remains quite still and self-contained.

Nothing happens. Something happens.
An outside police car's passing siren is a sound.

Goldsmiths, University of London, 18 July 1980

CERNE ABBAS

I

weapons clink in evening silence
leather creaks
a *centuria* of men from Apulia, Sicily and Provence
        in iron helmets and hob-nailed sandals
enter a green secluded valley

        corn, cattle, gold, silver and iron
        hides, slaves, and clever hunting dogs
        are what they've been sent here for

the Giant faces them
tall on his hill in the low northern light
his outline, chalk-white, incised in steep, springy turf
ancient, with upraised club and jutting phallus

2

five hundred years on, a missionary to the Saxons
spirit ablaze with the glory and mercy of Christ
walks the same road, bringing news of salvation
glad tidings of the triumph of daylight

night is coming on, but he feels his faith to be
a light militant that can defeat all darkness

the villagers pelt him with mud, fasten
a cow's tail to his arse, and chase him away

as he washes off the filth at a nearby spring, he sees
a vision of God in His radiance and falls to his knees

night gathers on the downs
the Giant looms on the hill

3

came via Dorchester, turned off at Hardy's statue
then drove up the valley and parked the car

here we stand in sunshine among cottages –
        stone, half-timber, white stucco, or brick –
flowers framing their doorways,
the downs tall and green at their backs

        the Giant
        leans over the village

each evening, century after century,
the villagers lock their doors
        against darkness and silence
and light small lamps against nightfall

4

sheep-cropped turf
a thorn tree high on the down
a National Trust fence encloses the Giant
below the iron-age earthwork on the prow of the hill

    silence
    evening light
    a whisper of wind in thickets of gorse

four-square but diminutive from this distance
the church raises its tower
shepherd-like above a huddle of colloquial roofs

our car
small in the faraway car park

5

the Giant may not, of course, be pre-Roman
Roman perhaps
or mediaeval
or even later than that

    first mention:
    for repareing ye Giant 3 shillings
    (churchwarden's records, 1694)

we have a laugh –
    such a diligent, un-partisan churchwarden! –
as we get into the car,
close the doors and drive away

6

sheep-cropped turf
thorn tree high on the hill

gnarled roots
deep in the chalky earth

black limbs tremble
in the wind off the downs

green leaves
catching the last of the light

AVEBURY

The stones stand enormously in their circle.
The village houses huddle together.

In the morning, open the curtains wide:
the stones are curious, they want to see

the salt cellar seated beside the egg cup,
the tall white cartons standing to attention,

the loaf placed firmly on the table,
the kettle breathing its plume of steam.

Step out of the house. A misty day.
From the corner of your eye catch a glimpse

of looming twin sarsens, gruff ancients
conversing with a whispering beech tree.

Get better acquainted with a particular stone,
its protrusions, roughness, fissures and crevices,

trace with your eye the avenues of monoliths
as they march off into the weather.

Someone is following you now with intent to speak.
Look around. Only tall stones leaning in mist.

Greet them, these stone personages. The moment's
important word is on the tip of your tongue

unspoken. Wordless, always just about to begin,
your householder's colloquy with age-old silence.

EMPIRES

rice farmers, woodcutters, fishermen
saké brewers and sellers of radishes
bean curd makers, minor feudal retainers
noodle stall owners and mendicant priests

emerged in 1868
into a brave new world of empires

a hundred years on, snagged
on a thorn tree branch
        beside a stony Himalayan path,
an empty Mitsubishi fertiliser sack

flips and flaps, a new kind of prayer flag
legislating in the mountain wind

SPARROW

I

I sit in the launderette doorway
reading a paperback anthology
        as I wait for the cycle to finish

planes pass overhead, one each ninety seconds
descending steadily to Heathrow
sucking kerosene from wing-tanks to feed their engines
bringing thousands each hour to their landfall

a seventeenth-century voice meanwhile numbers
the kisses beyond number he wants from Celia:

> *Adde a thousand, and so more*
> *Till you equall with the store*
> *All the grasse that Rumney yeelds*
> *Or the sands in Chelsey fields*

Catullus Englished
Libya's desert sands transposed
to lush Kentish pasture and Chelsea's pebbled shore

a few pages more, a hundred years on:

> *This Casket* India's *glowing Gems unlocks*
> *And all* Arabia *breathes from yonder Box*

a different leaf from the Roman codex
some bankable new lines in imported goods

> (in the Directors' Court Room,
>   in East India House on Leadenhall Street,
> a bas-relief: *Britannia Receiving the Riches of the East*)

some pages more, another hundred years:

Measure the course of that sulphur orb that lights the darksom day
Set stations on this breeding Earth & let us buy and sell

2

       … till you equal each brick and tile
       In Lots Road's tow'ring chimneyed pile
       (Near where the Thames doth ebb and flood
       O'er Chelsea Creek's sour sheeted mud)
       Or all the coal therein devoured
       So London Transport may be powered,
       Or the yield of cash-quick crops
       That superseded Romney's flocks,
       Where now the shielded Magnox core
       Affrights poor Dungeness's shore …

3

Wide-fuselage, low-wing design, four podded under-wing turbofan engines, developing between 264 and 276KN of thrust. Fuel tanks in the wings and tail-plane, reserve fuel tanks in the outer wing sections. Maximum fuel capacity: 216,840 litres.

Cruise speed 900 kph. Range 7,200 nautical miles. On a flight of 3,500 miles carrying 56,700 kilograms of fuel, it will consume an average of five gallons (19 litres) per mile.

4

round-hulled, single-masted
        square-sailed, double-ruddered vessels
ride at anchor off the port of Ostia

blessed Plenty pours her brimming horn

from Egypt: wheat, marble, ivory and slaves
from Britain: tin, lead, pigs and oak
from Spain: gold, silver, copper, fish paste, olive oil and wine

blessed Plenty pours her brimming horn

seventeen hundred years on
and the vernal gale fills the swelling sail
        of an Indiaman rounding the Cape
(cotton, silk, linen, indigo, saltpetre, tea)

blessed Plenty pours her brimming horn

and now at Heathrow, Jumbos –
        long-haul from margins to metropolis –
disgorge stacked pallets
onto oil-stained concrete and asphalt aprons

blessed Plenty pours her brimming horn

while, emerging from First Class at Terminal Three
to the bows and smiles of the flight attendants

blessed Plenty pours her brimming horn

here come our new accountants of unquenchable desire –
        men in expensive shoes
        whose briefcases hold the future

5

young William Blake
walking south one day to Dulwich, saw
a mulberry tree
with *bright angelic wings bespangling every bough like stars*

    angels on Peckham Rye?
    who might see those now?

alabaster skin, faint blue stains below her eyes
a young girl runs and skips in sunshine
on the pavement outside the launderette

and she coughs from time to time
and it's bronchial
comes from deep inside her body's smallness

    (the planes pass overhead, one
    each ninety seconds,
    descending steadily to Heathrow)

in the forecourt of the adjacent house –
home to five cracked flower pots,
three dustbins and a struggling tree –

a sparrow, all feathers and brio,
swerves in flight
and lands on a branch with a *cheep*

August 1980

IX

ALTITUDE

> *nil mortalibus ardui est* (Horace, *Odes* 1.3)

we sit in rows in a vibrating aluminium tube
Muzak wafts from speakers to sugar our anxiety
the hatches are sealed shut
    doors to automatic please
we're about to be projected by kerosene into very thin air

we turn onto the runway
and power is slipped from its leash

    (Greeks, Phoenicians
        setting keel to breakers
    putting out across the elemental sea)

brass pots, swords and ploughshares
    cantilever spans and Rolls-Royce engines
we delve in the world and wrench it to our purposes
the Tibetans were right
when they made their blacksmiths outcasts

    but: there's no way out except one

and so in the end one says *yes*
and arrives at 30,000 feet
exulting despite onerself in the twentieth century

    after lunch, Anatolia:

wrinkled sun-burnt hills,
tiny cross-hatched fields in folded valleys

and a fierce blue lake
staring up from inside its rim of crusted salt
at our sliver of edged metal
flying far too high to cast a shadow

WAKING

the window of blank awakening

    the pattern holds good
    weeds spring up on the sill

the unanswerable landscape reassembles
in an instant
to what we always knew

and we go down
from the empty places, to walk

    the ruined valleys, inhabit
    the abrasive cities

delight despite ourselves
with only naked consciousness to clothe us

AL FINTAS

a breeze-block café under the stars
somewhere to eat on the edge of a desert
cooking smells drift through warm night air

red carpets spread in front of the door
paraffin lamps placed on sand
men in dishdashas recline on cushions
sipping smoke from bubbling shishas

the owner comes from his kitchen, bearing
a glowing lump of charcoal held in tongs
he moves to and fro like a night nurse
tending to the pipes of his patients

    a hospice for an old dispensation
    lingering here a little longer yet

twenty yards away
beyond a shimmering wire-mesh fence
the six-lane highway floods past, headlights glaring

who could doubt the solid funded presence
        here where the Company extends
its steel spider-work out to sea
to feed the restless queue of tankers

but the swallows
        the green taste of Europe still upon them
passing through in swift lilting flight
above hot sand and tidemark

heartbeat
        under feathers
the small precisely navigating brain
behind each pair of small black eyes

messengers who
        arouse the doubt that
saves us, who bring us back to
our senses

to sandbanks and spits
        to the little clusters of offshore rocks
all recent superstructures
tentative again

DESERT SUN, WIND FROM THE NORTH

Qasr as Sabiyah, Kuwait, October 1980

camels graze
on ochre-yellow desert below
an escarpment of fractured sandstone

in the distance, black tents,
air conditioners bolted to their poles
pickup trucks parked outside them

wind and sun, silence
but for the faint throb of generators
intermittent on the breeze

some miles further, no more tents or trucks
just desert and a horizon-bound road,
hot sand sifting across black tarmac

and then, at the peninsula's end, a building:
the expensive road came all these miles
to a concrete box with a policeman in it

to a beach of banked white seashells
to the rusted skeleton of a ship
stranded on an empty foreshore

where shoals of mudskippers
skitter across the tidal flats
with startled eyes and popping mouths

where buzzards perch on grass tufts
unmoving, unblinking,
bolts of lightning gloved in feathers

where, if you listen carefully, you can hear
the rumble of the Iraqi guns
pulverising Iranians in Khorramshahr
and all along the Shatt al-Arab waterway

READING HORACE IN KUWAIT

pone sub curru nimium propinqui
solis in terra domibus negata (Odes 1.22)

1

brief February rains
gun-grey sky above a suddenly half-green desert
cloudbursts
      splashes of watery sunlight
flare stack flames reel in a gusty wind

2

in a leafy glade –
hush, soft grass and summer flowers,
      an Italy drowned in rural quietness
far from the rigours and alarms
of the empire's desert borders

      where the sun steers close and
      mile on mile is uninhabited heat –

Horace is wandering
beyond the bounds of his Sabine farm
singing of Lalage, his *sweet chatterer*

when he meets a wolf
      (Parthia feeds no beast that size
      Africa, nurse of monsters, breeds lesser lions)
which at once turns tail –

the fierce un-Roman world

> *parched Numidia or*
> *Syrtes' burning sands*

disarmed
on meeting *a good man innocent of sin*

3

twenty years before
the legions led by Crassus
    had crossed the Euphrates on a bridge of boats
flights of Parthian arrows flickered through the air
and hardly a man came back

a flash flood
sluices down a wadi, runs into sand
and vanishes without a trace

IN THE EMIRATE

His Highness the Amir Jaber al-Ahmad al-Jaber al-Sabah
today visited

    heaps of sand
    roadside concrete detritus
    stacks of splintery four-foot laths

Kuwait's three famous water towers
(the largest contains a million gallons of water)

    shovels, pickaxes
    a snout-nosed yellow digger
    cheap boots and dusty overalls

which take the form of
the perfumed water-spraying equipment

    dinar wages
    saved week by week
    sent home (Yemen, Balochistan) once a quarter

used by Kuwaiti people in the past
at wedding parties and on social occasions

on the way to Kuwait City
        we drive through Hawalli
a Palestinian neighbourhood

        battered low-rise buildings
        broken windows
        rubbled streets and potholed tarmac

so *this* is where my students live ...

in English composition classes
        in the air-conditioned training centre
the Palestinian students have just one topic
although many ways to voice it:

        the olive trees, the orange groves
        the empty well, the big iron key
        the deeds to the house
        in a box under a bed in a camp in Lebanon

Khalil apologises for yesterday's absence from class
his first son was being born

        congratulations, warmest congratulations!
        what are you going to call him?

Balfour, he says, looking me straight in the eye

CAIRO

an avenue of tattered palm trees
a line of dilapidated horse-drawn carriages
conservatories with shattered panes of glass
the past now looks like this

the present is a run-down power plant
broken blackened window grilles
grimy walls and thirty-watt bulbs
an incessant clamour of machines

a crumbling government building
guarded by teenage conscripts
with Kalashnikovs and bayonets
disconsolate among heaped sandbags

a bus terminus at night
a maze of concrete walkways
small figures hurrying through the shadows
to elbow themselves onto shuddering buses

a small park, muddy underfoot, where rain
drips from palm trees onto stalls
selling second-hand English textbooks
marketing management medicine maths

the young men leafing through them –
the aspiration, the earnestness
the almost impossible odds –
what futures will flow from this

THE FAVOURS

Market

heaped fruit, leather bags, wickerwork baskets
bolts of fabric, dangling lamps and brasswork
ironmongers, 'suppliers of steel tools and small engines'
packed trams clanging through crowds and traffic

muddy side streets seethe with industry
(wood, reed, beaten metal)
furniture makers plane planks out on the pavement
(rococo chairs stand fastidiously in the gutter)

high blue sky
jumbled skyline
fading peeling tattering crumbling walls
a child totters happily along the pavement in her pyjamas

the earth hath He appointed for His creatures
which is it of the favours of your Lord that ye deny?

Café

sawdust floor, cracked marble counter
brown-spotted mirrors, rickety chair
a cat, asleep in the sun on the windowsill,
wakes, stretches, comes to sit under my table

the muezzin calls from across the street,
melismatic and vibrato-laden,
quartertones curdled with electronic distortion
loud enough to make the windows rattle

an old, old man in blue robe and white headcloth
brings me water
and a round steel platter laden
with chickpeas, salad and bread

the earth hath He appointed for His creatures
wherein are fruit and sheathed palm trees
husked grain and scented herb
which is it of the favours of your Lord that ye deny?

Mosque

hundred-foot walls, a soaring portal
stone steps up from street to doorway
a dark low-ceilinged corridor, then out
into a four-square courtyard – look up!

carved fleurs-de-lis crown the walls
shreds of cloud drift across a square of blue
stone magnificence frames the shifting sky
I never expected the scale of this

the sun and the moon are made punctual
the stars and the trees adore
and the sky He hath uplifted
which is it of the favours of your Lord that ye deny?

he has had centuries to get acquainted
with the goddess on his ceiling

feet in the east, hands in the west
Nut gives birth to the sun each day

mother of gods and mistress of ritual
she is the river of the sky

her overarching belly is filled with stars
her breasts will sweeten nothingness

she extends her arms towards him
from the ceiling of the world

but can never reach him
here in the house of the dead

PALEOPAPHOS

ubi amor ibi oculis est

I

a scuffed patch of mosaic in the dust
some annotated chunks of greyish stone

a small white village
        sunk in sun and silence
beyond the perimeter fence

        once the greatest
        temple of Aphrodite in the whole Greek world

to fence things off for preservation
is one method of neglect

2

nightly rituals
of the seafront disco dance floor

see! her chosen single couple

        each move
        of hand or hip or thigh
                of fingertip or foot, each
        answering glance of eye

says the sacred space is always
here
        in the dance of those who choose
to set foot within her sphere

3

moment by moment
        arising from the world
blown spray in the wind from off the sea

you break us open again and again

he came to her bed:

        he had not thought that life
        would hold such glory for him

4

a cool, salty, insistent breeze
        comes in over the wave crests
dances
among ruffled hair at forehead and nape

        white cliffs
        a curve of bay

absence so great
it has the taste of presence

        shivering up the spine

again and again
born out of restlessness, nothingness

        the glittering sea

MONASTERY IN CYPRUS

dry friable earth
where fields step down to the sea

a cloister
a small perfection of rhyming arches
a circular pool
spring water runs over a lip of stone

        the slow flow of prayer

hidden from the world
raised by hand for the love of God
a courtyard which quietly breathes the sky –
second by second
            water's silvery tinkle
the constant small inventions of peace

chapel with its friendly barrel roof
courtyard with its glancing swallows

crepuscular interior
            lit with the glint of candles
and the memory of countless small devotions

little dynamo half-buried in a hillside
little cave of darkness, icons and patriarchs

little snail, little snail shell
creeping down the centuries

            teach us
            how to be insouciant, obscure and happy
            teach us how

so untendentiously to maintain the sacred

MELTEMI

the Aegean grinds its teeth on a shelf of pebbles
yachts fret at anchor in a fierce blue swell

a speedboat whinges and spatters across the bay
its clamour gusting in and out of focus on the wind

in the new-built hotel doors slam open and shut
and windows rattle in their frames

    (but the road to the old village
    is hushed, a dappled
    tunnel of ancient olive trees)

after sunset we take
the zigzag path up the mountain
to naked granite, to wind and darkness

where we lie on our backs
on the still warm stone, and watch
the sky silt up with a million grains of starlight

Santorini, 1981

FOUR

(1981–1991)

X

ON ARRIVAL

city lights glitter
        from horizon to horizon
the plane descends

...

stainless steel slatted ceiling
immaculate high-sheen floor

changing money
        notes and coins
come across the counter in a little plastic tray

looking for the exit –
                oh, right!
in Japan *first floor* means ground floor

...

plastic-wrapped slippers
tissues in a 'leather' dispenser
disposable razor, disposable toothbrush
shower cap, clothes brush, shoe horn, emergency torch

        everything in its place

a slot machine sells magazines in the lobby
the green tea dispenser dispenses green tea in the corridor

...

narrow streets
printing presses in rickety wooden workshops

an ornamental lake, stepping stones and carp
a gravel path between dark trees

outside the subway station
        a just-under-life-size
smiling plastic statue of Colonel Sanders

…

in the underground concourse, a
cascade of commuters pours over
        the lip of the staircase
filling the passage from wall to wall

    no sound but

the shuffle and flap of
shoe soles on polished floor

…

north from the city
        deep winding valleys
sombre with ranked cedars

the bus rounds a curve:
concrete, turbines, transformers and sluice gates

pylons head off
in easy strides over mountains in four directions

a small rain-wet graveyard
holds its own by the grassy verge

...

stone tank at the top of wet stone steps
pour water on the hands, rinse the mouth
bow, toss coins in the slatted box
clap to call the god's attention

a deep drum booms among shadowy pines

...

two-ring gas range
tile-floored bathroom
        (wooden bucket and re-heatable tub)
six-mat living room
balcony with a reputed view of Mount Fuji

in the local shopping area:
        pink tinsel street hangings
and a loudspeaker on every lamp post

...

bookstore in Shinjuku
transcriptions of Ainu oral literature (whales and bears)

a sudden awareness of being in TOKYO
thirty million people, all consuming

Tokyo & Chichibu, 16–29 September 1981

1

switches: up is on, down is off
each night I turn my key the wrong way in the lock

入口 = entrance
出口 = exit
板橋本町 = my subway stop

2

Shinjuku, Shibuya
neon bite and semiotic flash:

pizza napoletana in a 'German' beer hall
        where a dapper five-piece band
is playing *Dear Old Dixie*

a ganja gangster film watched
        by intense young Japanese
in dreadlocks and Rastafarian hats

Laphroaig in a plastic space-age bar
        my glass embossed
with a bust of Goethe, his name and dates

(a peaty nostalgia
        for what things 'really' mean
smoulders in the glass and on the tongue)

3

the first post arrives from England
familiar words
familiar names on airmail paper
these too start to slip away from what I thought they meant

    six mats and a sliding door
    looking out over miles of rooftops
    to a sunset behind Mount Fuji

       loneliness, says Abe Kōbō —
       an unsatisfied thirst for illusion

Ring Road No. 7 growls six floors below

this must be the place —

    the noncentre determined otherwise
    than as loss of centre

       signs without fault
       offered to an active interpretation

a locus where the meanings start to play

Tokyo, 29 September 1981

KOMACHI

Ōta Shōgo's Komachi Fuden *performed*
by the Tenkei Gekijō Theatre Company

an old woman is crossing a bridge by twilight
centimetre by centimetre she's approaching her death

a flock of ghosts shuffle behind her
her furniture stacked high on their backs

she steps off the bridge and sits down to rest
the ghosts assemble her house around her, then vanish

she sits like a sotoba, like a tree-stump, like a stone
among battered cupboards and torn paper screens

she cooks instant noodles on a small charcoal stove
it takes for ever, suddenly she slams a cupboard door

she winds up a gramophone and puts on Edith Piaf
an officer in whites appears and shimmers before her

the record ends, the suitor vanishes
the old woman eats her noodles

a doctor and a nurse tiptoe towards her
when they reach her they find that she's dead

the ghosts return and dismantle the house
a clumsy ballet of capering wardrobes and tables

now no one and nothing is here
except for an old woman and her gramophone

she will never move again – but then she stirs
she winds up the gramophone but no sound comes out

she moves to the bank of the river
and kneels at the edge of everything

she cups her hands and drinks
quenching solitude with knowledge of solitude

STRAW AGAINST THE WINTER

pine trees
stepping stones bedded in moss

a partly open gate
a temple garden glimpsed –
          grass, rocks, shrubs and gravel
wooden pillars, creamy plaster, grey-tiled roof
an open door, a seated monk half-seen –

the thin drone of a chanted sutra floats
          through chilly air,
from time to time the monk
twitches the shoulder of his garment straight

          deep note of a bell

brilliant red yellow orange
leaves shiver down
          to bone-dry frosty earth
to fade in brittle grey-brown heaps

a thread of water spills
from mossy ledge to rippled pool

...

wind rushes through
tree tops, thrums
in power lines and pylons

thickets of bamboo
swirl, bushy heads
dishevelled in the wind

a sheltering cliff
quiets three pine trees to a
local stillness, harbours

an unruffled Jizō
red-bibbed in his sandstone niche
beside the trodden path

...

a stone tank fed by
a trickle from a bamboo pipe

      a tin cup with a bamboo handle
      rests on the chiselled rim

the temple bell hangs from its beam –
      two tons of silence
dense with centuries of reverberation

beside shuttered wooden buildings
      gardeners crouch, fingers working fast,
planting bulbs in loamy earth

the trunks of the trees
already wrapped
in straw against the winter

Kamakura, 21–22 November 1981

ZUISENJI GARDEN

pool
black wind-ruffled water

an island
          two small bridges
yellow sandstone cliff
large shallow cave

dry winter season
          brown gully
the memory of a waterfall

the garden is simply made up of two elements
rocks and water
this concealed beauty of the garden
enchants us very much

          unimpressive
          unexciting

sustaining
in its taste of nothing

absence of flavour which haunts the tongue

ALL THAT FLOWS

a tunnel cut through stone that leads to
a corridor of vermilion torii that leads to
a sunlit hollow among wooded cliffs

      ferns, a pool, a waterfall
      a red bridge to a tiny shrine
      a cast-iron incense pot, from which
      smoke coils up in slanting sunlight

in a dark cave
water ripples from a spring
through stone tanks where, it's said, washing
your money will double it

candles flicker
bells dangle from coloured streamers

      eggs offered on altars
      an image of a woman-headed snake:
      Benten (Sarasvati) – goddess of
          music, water, time and eloquence

pellucid tones
      of flute and koto
spill softly from speakers at the tea house door

Zeniarai Benten, Kamakura

ZAZEN FOR FOREIGNERS

with Nishijima-sensei

after instructions for posture:

> *you need not think anything*
> *you need not feel anything*
> *just by sitting we*
> *penetrate to the foundation of the Buddha's teachings*

(pause)

> *are there any questions?*

after zazen a lecture:

the Buddha's four philosophies
can be equated (in terms of Western philosophical logic) thus:

1. *agony*	=	*idealism (thought/intellect)*
2. *aggregation*	=	*materialism (feeling/senses)*
3. *action/non-consciousness*	=	*realism/existentialism*
4. *reality*	=	*reality itself: <u>not</u> philosophy*

> he writes the word DIREKTIC on the blackboard

Hegel's dialectic encompasses
the first three philosophies but remains theory
realise the fourth philosophy (reality) first, and then the first three become

> *extremely clear*

> *sitting in quietness only*

> *the Buddha realised the splendid world*

> *I can say yes and no at the same time*

VISITING IAN IN PRISON

he's pale and thin and drawn
his arm in a sling

RULES OF THE PRISON:

> *don't escape*
> *don't kill yourself*
> *don't speak* (and forty-six more)

when I come out after an hour
I feel I've been inside for months

blue sky, an uncanny quietness
sunlight on white railings in the car park
salt wind, the tang of seaweed
a small stream rippling in a concrete channel

> the sudden quenching
> of a thirst I didn't know I'd had

'I haven't seen the sky for seven weeks
and the food comes in through a hole in the door'

tethered boats, coiled ropes, heaped nets
mooring lines quiver and plash –
outside the harbour the sea runs fiercely
climbing sandstone cliffs in sheets of spray

at the inn, fish in teriyaki sauce,
hot saké, half a crab each, white rice
and yellow pickles, brought to us by
Mrs Watanabe in her cheerful apron

...

clear morning
a high winding path with sudden views down to
blue sea
curdling to white around rocks

grey canted roofs tucked into narrow valleys
(scales on a cubist snake)
boats drawn up on slipways
undulating offshore loops of floating buoys

pine logs for growing mushrooms
are stacked beside the path, slivers of
rust-red bark
scattered on the forest floor

the dirt track descends through
woods to the village, where
in terraced fields
edged with yellow straw

fat, white-domed
green-tufted daikon protrude
six inches above
Mr Watanabe's black and finely sifted soil

IN IZU (2)

sunset, mountain road –
the yellow digger rests its
knuckle on the ground

GLIMPSING THE GARDEN

tea ceremony at Kenninji, Kyoto

green-and-white rectangular cakes
yellow confections shaped like birds

shaved wooden spikes to eat them
    (bark left on at the upper end)

gold clouds swirl
        on a black lacquer tea caddy
whose lid is removed to reveal

    an astonishment of green powdered tea

the cup placed before you   bow
move it to one side   bow   to the other side   bow
raise it   rotate it   take a sip

deliciously bitter, rich in texture

    the pattern in the glaze
    begins to gleam through green froth
    as the tea is drunk

meanwhile, intermittent
    slight rearrangements
of objects around the charcoal hearth

    (attention!)

sliding screens are
        shot open for a
glimpse of garden then shot closed again

SANJŪSANGEN-DŌ

(the thirty-three-niche hall)

inside the 120-metre long
        shed-like building
(exterior wooden walls almost black)

the spirit of thunder
        (eyeballs, muscles, torso,
        dumb-bells, a whirling circle of drums)
and the spirit of the winds
        (snout, tusks, knotted scarf,
        a bulging bag athwart his shoulders)

and then the twenty-eight guardians, who carry
wheels swords bells drums bows arrows flutes and lutes
their heads encircled with haloes of fire

and one hundred rows of gold-leaf statues
each face crowned with
        ten more faces inside a spiky halo

and in the centre
the Bodhisattva sits on a golden lotus
        (carved by Tankei – 'at his late age of 82')
saving numberless worlds with her rippling forest of arms

a priest in black, green and white vestments
recites a sutra and dings his bell

        preserve me, I pray, from all obstacles
        for the sake of all sentient beings

smoke spirals from incense bowls

a candle flickers in the gloom
to the fleeting honour of Kannon

FOUR POSTCARDS FROM KYOTO

Saihōji

stones
          embedded in moss
water slips between
             banks of moss
under lichened trees
               the glow of moss
over dark water a footbridge
              smothered in moss

faintly, from the temple hall
a chanted sutra, the
thum thum thum thum, exactly regular, of a drum

      donnggg! of a large bronze bell

two old men sweep leaves

…

Philosopher's Walk

dark evening at the canal side
      (blossoming trees and falling petals)
an old man surrounded by
        a scrum of firemen
in fire-resistant suits and silver helmets

      the old man narrates, with
      shocked, unhappy gestures

the firemen prod with sticks
the smouldering skeleton of a yakitori stall
interrogate with their flashlights
        each blackened cranny
of what was, until ten minutes ago, a livelihood

...

Nanzenji

painted golden screens:

a tiger prowls beneath green splashes of bamboo
a tiger leaps, extends a ripple of tail
a red-tongued tiger laps from a swirl of water
a whirlpool of curled-up tiger sleeps and dreams

the shoji are open
the wooden veranda looks out on
a miniature ocean with its scaled-down archipelago

        stones
                        moss
                                        raked sand
            and clipped pines

behind the temple
        a red-brick aqueduct:
slick black water sluices between dank trees

...

Ryōanji

fifteen rocks sunk in five
pools of green-brown moss

enter stage assistants, set up rustic gate and zigzag fence, retire through upstage sliding door

enter Kogō, enter maidservant, young-woman masks, sumptuous orange robes

sit

enter landlady, long blue robe, no mask, long white headdress, sing-song speech, opens gate, speaks, closes gate, long slender fingers

Kogō and maid turn towards each other slowly, voices muffled by masks, drummers pick up drums, *plok plik* PLOK

sparse drum beats, flute begins then stops, muffled voices from behind masks, landlady withdraws through sliding door, flute sounds, slowly Kogō and maid turn, face audience again

drum
flute
voice

enter Nakakuni, white socks, gliding walk, bulbous blue-gold costume, speaks chantingly to musicians' chant and drums

chorus pick up fans, eight voice belly song, Nakakuni approaches gate, chorus put down fans, Nakakuni speaks, Kogō answers, maid stands, opens gate, returns and sits, Nakakuni steps to gate

Kogō speaks, Nakakuni recoils from gate

voice
drum
flute

Nakakuni sits by downstage pillar

enter stage assistants, fold up fence, remove it, remove gate, adjust Nakakuni's costume, exit through sliding door

Nakakuni moves to centre stage, bows, speaks, opens fan, places letter on fan, approaches Kogō, kneels, presents letter, withdraws, Kogō reads letter

voice
drum
flute

Nakakuni turns to face stage-front, adjusts one sleeve, adjusts the other, kneels

breathing

Nakakuni rotates with infinite slowness to face Kogō, looks, rotates with infinite slowness back again

flute
voice
drum

silence

Nakakuni stands, picks up fan, Kogō places reply on fan, Nakakuni steps back, puts reply in his clothing, slow dance, flute and drum, gliding diagonal steps, sudden swirl of sleeves, slow opening of the fan, sudden stamp of one foot, of the other foot, further glidings, stamp STAMP pause

Nakakuni speaks, chorus chants, Nakakuni departs from stage, arrives at curtain, whirls and stamps, shrill of flute

Kogō rises to her feet, stands, leans forward, no movement, looks

gets slowly off
the bus
bent in his brown

suit almost double
with age and
rheumatism into

a mark of
interrogation
of the pavement

from which
he picks a
cigarette

end he throws
with impatience
into the roadside

shrubs

BASHŌ: HAIKU

look carefully
shepherd's purse
flowering in the hedge

this road
with no one going along it
autumn evening

winter seclusion
again adjust
my back to this door post

young sparrows
answering voices
a nest of baby mice

morning dew
dirty cool
muddy melon

lightning!
out of darkness
a night heron's cry

SOME CULTURAL UNCERTAINTIES

Mr and Mrs Takasaki live next door
they have no English, I have scanty Japanese
we meet on the path
we laugh and wave our hands
and bow at every juncture

although of course

        one
        never
        knows

a gaffe that elsewhere might produce
a blood feud lasting generations
will here just possibly lead to

a barely perceptible
                      widening
                              of the
                                    eyes

        one hair
        on the head
        of the universe
        out of place

and the whole damn thing will never work again

AIR

wherever you turn
you are surrounded by language
like the air

John James

of course there are problems
such as being able to ask the way but not
being able to understand the answer

and people
in the trauma of having to speak to a
Foreigner
sometimes freeze into a statue named Panic

but in trains I pass the time
trying to pick my way through the adverts
spiky katakana, thickets of kanji
the looped lianas of graceful hiragana

in bars and restaurants
I am an inscrutable but baffled eavesdropper

but mostly I thread the trails of the city
carrying my own language in my head
carefully, like a pitcher of water brought
from a great distance without spilling a drop

taking care to maintain that balance,
breathing an unaccustomed air

CLIMBING, DESCENDING

I

breakfast at six a.m.
in a hut on a saddle between
two peaks

        in pale pink dawn-light
                mother-of-pearl mist
        swirls up from the valley

out: traverse a snowfield, ascend
a boulder-filled gully and then a spur –
        dangling chains and
        steel ladders bolted to rock –

to the scarp above, where
        a matted carpet of gnarled
fir-like bushes hugs the stony ground

        gloves on, a piercing wind

razorback ridges
        no clean rock face anywhere
everything broken, spiky, splintered
a precipitous wasteland
        mottled with snow patches,
furrowed and streaked with snow-filled gullies

        mist from the valleys
        licks and curls at the peaks

a cornice
(impressive even in its springtime dotage)
beetles over a snowfield

finally! sit in eddying cloud on the summit –
blue sky in patches, peaks
        appear, disappear in mist –
brew coffee, sip from the finger-warming mug

        in the silence of
        high mountains, the *beep* of an
        electronic watch

2

leave at dawn from the highest hut

muted first light, keen
wind across the snowfield

traverse to a broken ridge

swallows' wings whistle as
they curve and skim above snow

toil across scree to a terrace of boulders

snow smudges cupped in
north-facing crannies

drop down into the valley's curve

trees bigger as the path descends
the river little by little noisier

pass below crags, pass beside water

'mountains & rivers'
a traveller in a landscape scroll

jump, hop, skip, and step to the other bank

the river tumbles in its bed
boulder to white rounded boulder

follow the tree-lined riverbank path

> *turbulent confluence of*
> *two ice-cold waters*

wild flowers, green meadow

> *walk the grass of paradise*
> *in a sweat-soaked tee-shirt*

valley lodge

> *step softly on pinewood floors*
> *to an eight-tatami room*

yesterday's peak

> *looks in through the window*
> *from high above the trees*

Kamikochi, 3–4 July 1982

CHANGING, UNCHANGED

In the small town by the sea, last seen years ago,
concrete has replaced weathered wood,
a car park has been built on the fishermen's dock –
but the temple maintains its gravitas.

Shady paths newly gravelled and fenced,
young saplings planted among venerable cedars,
but in the old caves carved in the sandstone cliff
past pieties still speak in the silence.

The garden is turning towards autumn:
a maple tree with a single red branch,
a fading lawn, a rectangular bed of yellowing reeds,
a brisk wind ruffling evergreen bushes

as it scrambles uphill to the abbot's quarters –
and at the back of all this, an eroding cliff
from an era long before temples and gardens:
geology fringed with dark hanging pines.

In the museum, the metamorphosis of a tree trunk,
untouched but for two small faces carved in it:
someone saw Kannon and child in a tree stump,
incised a few notches and, wonderfully, left it at that.

Also: a green bronze mirror,
circular on its intricate wooden base,
dim with patina, reflecting nothing –
the full moon rising from a carved sea of clouds.

BON-ODORI IN KABUKICHŌ

in a concrete square under floodlights
to the beat of three drummers on a scaffolding platform
to a melody repeated from crackling loudspeakers
the old women in their summer kimonos are dancing
circling and circling the makeshift stage

> *step forward, step back*
> *hands sketch a rooftop in air*
> *hands make a small turning-inside-out gesture*
> *hands held up, palms facing each other*
> *clap clap clip-clap clap*
> *step forward*
> *step back*
> *a little dip of the body*
> *steady, graceful and tireless*

on littered tarmac surrounded by love hotels and cinemas
under neon signs and posters of half-naked women
in the parish of gangsters and hucksters and pimps
they're dancing to welcome the revisiting dead

the old women in their immaculate kimonos
their hair done up neatly in buns
their hips aslant, slightly swaying,
their faces without expression

BOW, CLAP TWICE, AND PRAY

Ōagata-jinja, Inuyama

Wooded hills, rice fields and rain,
a torii, and then a gravel path through trees

to a vermilion shrine and its three
objects of veneration, found, not made:

a tree trunk forked at the base
with a notch where the wood divides;

the torso of a hollow tree, an oval orifice
where a branch once grew;

and an empty trunk curved smoothly around
the convolutions of its own interior.

Here, in a silence without contrivance,
in the spacious quietness of this place,

a generous spirit suggests her presence:
tutelar of the blood-warm folded darkness

in which bone coalesces, eyeball swims to shape
and flesh reaches out to be small fingers.

A woman, thirty-five or forty years old,
walks with quick steps across the gravel,

throws a coin into the slatted box,
bows, claps twice, and prays.

XI

HŌKOKUJI

for Chirone

1

swept tarmac, just-so houses
        manicured gardens
(they must have combed that moss)
trimmed hedge and bamboo fence

river in its concrete channel
rinsing and smoothing shaggy green weeds

carp drift and play against the current
orange backs arch into sunlight

we stroll up the hill
        in pristine light
to the tree-shaded temple gateway

2

wave pattern in raked sand
very particular pine trees
we climb stone steps to the hall

a fume of incense, a seated Buddha
lacquer, gold, a clutter of objects for holy use
two unwavering candle flames

3

the garden is
river boulders, pine trees, moss

and a sort of elongated red cabbage
        planted here and there
in a whiteness of abstract gravel

        sublime nonsense
        asymmetrical exactness

boundless space in a few square feet

4

we sit on straw mats beside
the open sliding doors
to catch the faint cool breeze

        wooden steps
        a straw-wrapped pine tree

        dark bamboo grove
        a smoke of grey-green light

a paterfamilias crouches down outside
        attending to his camera
while three generations of his kin
line up for

        click!

the formal record of their visit

> *wabi is that incompleteness which in fact contains*
> *no thought of incompleteness*
>
> Sen no Sōtan: *Zencharoku*

a small hut in the shadow of a bamboo grove or among trees

mountains and rivers transplanted to your fireside

lay in charcoal and hang a kettle over it

restore the heart with old tea utensils

listen to the water in the kettle sing like the wind in the pines

watch the four seasons pass in a few square feet

let the waves of the river Wei flow from the dipper

draw straight from the source of heaven and earth

savour in your mouth the taste of the wind

KAGEKIYO

1

sleeping on wet grass
a far estuary our destination

rowing across the sea
a city of clouds in our dreams

late dewdrops waiting
for the morning wind to blow

2

blindness all blindness
one unending profitless darkness

a pine-bough hovel
a thin coat against winter winds
my body a framework of bones

> *listen*
> *listen now to the wind*
> *the wind in the pine trees on the hill*
> *snow is coming*
> *snow*

why must I wake from dreams
of flowers I cannot see?

> *listen*
> *listen now to the waves*
> *the waves running*
> *over rough stones to the cliff*
> *the evening tide is in*

my eyes cannot see autumn
but the wind brings news of a vanished past

3

they have beaten us in the mountains
and beaten us among the islands
and put us to flight at the passes –
how shall we defeat these Genji?

I landed alone on the beach
their massed ranks fled from my anger
how easy this killing is!
'I am Kagekiyo, captain of the Hei!'

sword points
and wild laughter on the battlefield

4

I am an old man
I have forgotten unforgettable things
a dragon grown old, outrun by village nags

my daughter
my daughter who never knew me
return to your home
my daughter, candle to my darkness
go on with your journey

sleeping on wet grass
rowing across the sea

distant river mouth
city of clouds

late dewdrops waiting
for the morning wind to blow

HIROSHIMA

1

The bomb fell rapidly and exploded after 43 seconds at an altitude of 580 metres. The blast stripped off clothing, tore off skin, and caused the rupture and explosion of intestines and other internal organs.

Wooden buildings within a radius of 2.3 kilometres were obliterated while those within 3.2 kilometres were half destroyed. Many people were trapped in their collapsed houses and were burned to death.

2

the grandeur of that cloud
        boiling up from the planet
in the morning sunlight

the hunger for apotheosis, for
the obliterating suddenness of the flash

    now I am become death, destroyer of worlds

as though
it would not be our own flesh which burnt

'when I took hold of her hand her skin came off like a glove'

3

the professor
was standing by the tram tracks near Miyuki Bridge
he was almost naked
clad only in his underpants
and was holding a rice ball in his right hand

beyond the tracks
the northern part of the city was a sea of fire

how
just then
and so many miles from his home
had he come to be holding a rice ball?

at that moment
he seemed a symbol of all
the modest aspirations of humankind

IFU BEACH, KUMEJIMA

1

shoreline waters glitter in sunlight
a sea heron stalks the shallows
dunlins scurry and probe at sea's edge
terns wheel and swerve

a skein of flickering birds' wings

    water's thin glaze
    over sand, reef and stone

2

eyes down to search for tokens
loving this shell and this one and this one

    the grace of these anonymous sarcophagi
    each an emblem
    of a life's urgent spiralling to order

licked clean now by the sea's salt tongue
haunted by echoes, empty as light

3

twisted swordfish at the tideline
fish corpses putrescent among driftwood
the huge deadweight of a turtle

flippers spreadeagled
burst black eyes
tangled entrails
black blood encrusting the sand

putrefying flesh
leaks from the great flaking dome of its shell

4

a hermit crab walks past my feet
travelling for miles across a few yards of sand

it walks precisely on its toes
        calciferous bundle on its back
having (it seems) a good enough idea of where it's going
overcoming every obstacle
beached driftwood or tangle of seaweed

        persistent inheritor
        purposeful migrant from pool to pool

walking the sea's edge in daylight

Grey roofs, blue roofs, red roofs, as far as the eye can see in morning sunlight. A twenty-year stubble of TV aerials. Concrete, wood frame, prefabricated panel; aluminium-railed balconies where bright bedding is displayed to sun and air.

How many shades of grey can you see, grey-white and white-grey, flecked with bits of green: a blurred wisp of bamboo, a brushstroke of pine, a smudge of bush, a speck of rooftop bonsai. Here the adolescent ungainliness of a northern palm tree, there an evergreen bush clipped to a disciplined roundness; or a pine tree with straw knee bandages, its limbs racked and bound on a frame of bamboo poles.

Trains passing over and under trains, at tangents, at right-angles, stitching the fabric of Tokyo; trains vanishing out of the corner of the eye beneath the strict entanglements of the power lines; trains bearing the providers to their sites of loyalty, attrition, and the wherewithal to live.

THE OLD LADY OF OGIKUBO

every time

I see her
in the
shopping street

very old
moving
very slowly

bent double
over her
walking stick

good
I think and
greet her

still alive

my name is Pat
my field is language acquisition
and I'm trying to find out
how Japanese children acquire directives

I have a lot of data
and there are a number of recurring patterns

for example
when a mother requests an action by a child
it usually comes with a reason why the child should comply

    because that's the way things are done
    because Mother wants you to do it
    because people will make fun of you if you don't

now I'm in a living room
and Aki-chan is eating a *mikan*, a Japanese orange
and her mother says: *Patricia-san says, 'I want some too'*

I've said no such thing

Aki-chan
the not-deaf child
studies me carefully from under her fringe

then holds out the *mikan* towards me

SASHIMI AND ROSES

red chunks of raw fish
nestle on a cloud of white grated daikon

a tiny mound of green mustard
one green leaf

the discretion of white wood chopsticks

    ocean-borne scent
    salt, sword edge and pine forest

sparseness and pale scrubbed wood
a slender vase with three red roses

and beneath it all

    the almost perceptible
    shifting of tectonic plates

(although it's better not to think about that)

VACUUM STORM

haiku by Natsuishi Ban'ya

that's my brain there
that gap between
those fleecy clouds

bare branches
tonight again the constellations
are full of misprints

cherry blossoms falling
newsprint drinks
great draughts of human blood

into the Sea of Japan
the lightning's tail
is plunged

rainbow
raise your ballerina's leg
over the Sea of Japan

pushed off the stairs
falling
I become a rainbow

diarrhoea
shitting electric wires, birds, fireworks
and clouds

sandstorm
head blown into
innumerable slopes

sometimes vacuums
sometimes clouds
pass through the lachrymal gland

the wind from the future
arrives
to cut the waterfall in two

over the gravestone shop on
the department store roof
radio waves fly

leaving the house for
a thousand years
at the door I hang a waterfall

the mountain range has ears
in the night
a stone is thrown

XII

MONUMENTA NIPPONICA

A Short History of Modern Japan

TOKYO
TOKYO
TOKYO
TOKYO
TOKYO
TOKYO
TOKYO
TOKYO
TOKYO
TOKYO
TOKYO
TOKYO
TOKYO
TOKYO
TOKYO
TOKYO
TOKYO
TOKYO
TOKYO
TOKYO
TOKYO
TOKYO
TOKYO
TOKYO
TOKYO
TOKYO
TOKYO
TOKYO
TOKYO
KYOTO

A Short History of Modern Japan

A Short Tour of Modern Japan

who?

It Is Not Perrmanent

flower

arrangemen

THE FOUR SEASONS IN TOKYO

spring

TOKYOTOKYOTOKYOTOKYOTOKYOTOKYOTOKYO
TOKYOTOKYOTOKYOTOKYOTOKYOTOKYOTOKYO
TOKYOTOKYOTOKYOTOKYOTOKYOTOKYOTOKYO
TOKYOTOKYOTOKYOTOKYOTOKYOTOKYOTOKYO
TOKYOTOKYOTOKYOTOKYOTOKYOTOKYOTOKYO
TOKYOTOKYOTOKYOTOKYOTOKYOTOKYOTOKYO
TOKYOTOKYOTOKYOTOKYOTOKYOTOKYOTOKYO
TOKYOTOKYOTOKYOTOKYOTOKYOTOKYOTOKYO
TOKYOTOKYOTOKYOTOKYOTOKYOTOKYOTOKYO
TOKYOTOKYOTOKYOTOKYOTOKYOTOKYOTOKYO
TOKYOTOKYOTOKYOTOKYO *cherry*   KYOTOKYO
TOKYOTOKYOTOKYOTOKYO   KYOTOKYO
TOKYOTOKYOTOKYOTOKYO *blosso* KYOTOKYO
TOKYOTOKYOTOKYOTOKYOTOKYOTOKYOTOKYO
TOKYOTOKYOTOKYOTOKYOTOKYOTOKYOTOKYO
TOKYOTOKYOTOKYOTOKYOTOKYOTOKYOTOKYO

m

m

m

summer

TOKYOTOKYOTOKYOTOKYOTOKYOTOKYOTOKYO
TOKYOTOKYOTOKYOTOKYOTOKYOTOKYOTOKYO
TOKYOTOKYOTOKYOTOKYOTOKYOTOKYOTOKYO
TOKYOTOKYOTOKYOTOKYOTOKYOTOKYOTOKYO
TOKYOTOKYOTOKYOTOKYOTOKYOTOKYOTOKYO
TOKYOTOKYOTOKYOTOKYOTOKYOTOKYOTOKYO
TOKYOTOKYOTOKYOTOKYOTOKYOTOKYOTOKYO
TOKYOTOKYOTOKYOTOKYOTOKYOTOKYOTOKYO
TOKYOTOKYOTOKYOTOKYOTOKYOTOKYOTOKYO
TOKYOTOKYOTOKYOTOKYOTOKYOTOKYOTOKYO
TOKYOTOKYOTOKYOTOKYO   AIR   KYOTOKYO
TOKYOTOKYOTOKYOTOKYO   KYOTOKYO
TOKYOTOKYOTOKYOTOKYO   CON   KYOTOKYO
TOKYOTOKYOTOKYOTOKYOTOKYOTOKYOTOKYO
TOKYOTOKYOTOKYOTOKYOTOKYOTOKYOTOKYO
TOKYOTOKYOTOKYOTOKYOTOKYOTOKYOTOKYO

TOKYOTOKYOTOKYOTOKYOTOKYOTOKYOTOKYO
TOKYOTOKYOTOKYOTOKYOTOKYOTOKYOTOKYO
TOKYOTOKYOTOKYOTOKYOTOKYOTOKYOTOKYO
TOKYOTOKYOTOKYOTOKYOTOKYOTOKYOTOKYO
TOKYOTOKYOTOKYOTOKYOTOKYOTOKYOTOKYO
TOKYOTOKYOTOKYOTOKYOTOKYOTOKYOTOKYO
TOKYOTOKYOTOKYOTOKYOTOKYOTOKYOTOKYO
TOKYOTOKYOTOKYOTOKYOTOKYOTOKYOTOKYO
TOKYOTOKYOTOKYOTOKYOTOKYOTOKYOTOKYO
TOKYOTOKYOTOKYOTOKYOTOKYOTOKYOTOKYO
TOKYOTOKYOTOKYOTOKYO   *e*   KYOTOKYO
TOKYOTOKYOTOKYOTOKYO *l*   KYOTOKYO
TOKYOTOKYOTOKYOTOKYO   *a* KYOTOKYO
TOKYOTOKYOTOKYOTOKYOTOKYOTOKYOTOKYO
TOKYOTOKYOTOKYOTOKYOTOKYOTOKYOTOKYO   *f*
TOKYOTOKYOTOKYOTOKYOTOKYOTOKYOTOKYO

winter

snowsnowsnowsnowsnowsnowsnowsnowsnow
TOKYOTOKYOTOKYOTOKYOTOKYOTOKYOTOKYO
TOKYOTOKYOTOKYOTOKYOTOKYOTOKYOTOKYO
TOKYOTOKYOTOKYOTOKYOTOKYOTOKYOTOKYO
TOKYOTOKYOTOKYOTOKYOTOKYOTOKYOTOKYO
TOKYOTOKYOTOKYOTOKYOTOKYOTOKYOTOKYO
TOKYOTOKYOTOKYOTOKYOTOKYOTOKYOTOKYO
TOKYOTOKYOTOKYOTOKYOTOKYOTOKYOTOKYO
TOKYOTOKYOTOKYOTOKYOTOKYOTOKYOTOKYO
TOKYOTOKYOTOKYOTOKYOTOKYOTOKYOTOKYO
TOKYOTOKYOTOKYOTOKYO   KYOTOKYO
TOKYOTOKYOTOKYOTOKYO   KYOTOKYO
TOKYOTOKYOTOKYOTOKYO   KYOTOKYO
TOKYOTOKYOTOKYOTOKYOTOKYOTOKYOTOKYO
TOKYOTOKYOTOKYOTOKYOTOKYOTOKYOTOKYO
TOKYOTOKYOTOKYOTOKYOTOKYOTOKYOTOKYO

FIVE

(1983–1995)

XIII

THE BLUE EDGE

for Chirone

I

from the beach you can see it
the line where the sea turns
from turquoise to cobalt
from coastal shelf to deep-sea trench

in face mask and snorkel we
swim out through shallows
gliding just above
a coral garden in full bloom

ochre brains bulbous on the seabed
pink branching vein-like intricacies
orange many-throated sponges
lavender-blue lungs draped over boulders

2

suddenly we reach the edge
a precipice where
the seabed drops away and we're left
hanging above

an abyss, into which
the imagination plummets –
that's much too deep! –
(the crush of billions of tons of blue …)

fish flit over the edge, silver sparks
vanishing
into depths beyond
daylight's reach or our cognisance

3

night
heavy limbs and sunburnt shoulders
salty tangled hair –
we lie in darkness, drifting

just above the surface of sleep
half-awake to
the *shooosh* of the sea beyond
the palm-frond walls, that will repeat

all night without our hearing it
as we float away from shore, suspended
above our own dark
unsounded places

Moalboal, Philippines

BEACH

Moalboal, Philippines

mounting towers of boiling cumulonimbus
processional
above the hills of Negros

but not going far
burning off before they can cross the water
to this white beach where
the sky's been blue for days

sun blaze on sea
ripples lisp on hot sand
hermit crabs scuttle or stay interminably still

I sit with barely a thought
in the shade of a palm-frond shelter

the sea breathes its colours
a peacock walking in the garden of the world
turning its feathers this way and that way
coruscating in the sunlight

never the same glint or flourish twice

    no blueprint
    no schedule

there's no such thing as chaos

POSEOKJEONG BOWER

Kyongju, South Korea

among pine trees
a dusty stone channel
raised a little above the level of the earth

where, on summer nights, poems
and cups of wine
were floated down with the current

until one evening the future arrived
uninvited
and a king fell on his sword

the stream still flows
its water now
too low to feed the sinuous granite channel

the palace gone, paddy fields surround
this accidental monument –
an epigram in

undulant curves of stone
on the themes of power, pleasure
and their passing

a trinket fallen
from a dynasty's pocket
in tall grass beside a country road

GINSENG WINE WITH MR KWON

Mr Kwon
in his white shorts
with his shock of short black hair and his glasses awry

Mr Kwon
with his sudden pronouncements
his outbursts of total merriment
his fierce one-thing-at-a-time concentration
his treatment of all people alike
and his perfect impatience with all linguistic impedimenta

fills my glass with ginseng wine
and gives me a piece of calligraphy, a Korean song, he says

what does it mean? I ask

he adjusts his glasses and sits up very straight:

*Mongols come Chinese come man goes man fights woman cries
Japanese come man goes maybe dies woman cries many wars Korea
many wars Americans come communists come many wars now 38-
line country divide man gone maybe dead woman cries this means
this song very sad song please sing*

WATCHING THE WORLD LIGHTWEIGHT
CHAMPIONSHIP ON TV WHILE EATING
DINNER IN A BULGOGI RESTAURANT IN
KYONGJU WITH CHIRONE

marinated beef sizzles over charcoal
the table is spread with reds and yellows and whites
an anthology of kimchi in small ceramic bowls

cross-cuts, zoom-ins and close-ups
        bloodied faces
                rivulets of sweat
assault and battery orchestrated
into three-minute episodes –
short, sharp variations on the theme of harm

        for *human* read *male*, says Chirone

as one of the fighters hits the canvas with a wallop
        and stays there
the referee crouched and counting
the audience screaming –
        and then the winner's glove is lifted high

next up:
the weather forecast

we raise our glasses in a toast
to several hundred miles of rain-filled cloud
last night's warm front
now moving quietly across north-east China

THREE STONE BUDDHAS

Kyongju, South Korea

weathered
      smudged with green lichen
sitting out the centuries
under pine trees in a walled enclosure

      soldiers in chain mail deploy
      among blossoming trees

last night in pelting darkness
rainwater drenched their heads and laps,
      sluiced off carved stone bases
into the loamy earth

      a peasant woman stoops
      in stifling heat to light a stick of incense

this morning, steam rises
      from warming branches, sunlight
dapples the statues' granular repose

      an ant carries a yellow
      leaf across a carpet of pine needles

three stone Buddhas
      sitting out the centuries
under pine trees in a walled enclosure

      snow grows like white moss
      all through a winter night

THE KINGDOM OF PAGAN

Pagan, Burma

an ochre plain
studded with temples and pagodas

     white elegances
     brick cubes and ornamented spires
     distant glints of gold

seven hundred years

nothing is left of
     the palm-frond houses
or the mansions of ornate carved wood

only the brick and stone remain:
Buddhas in their caves of masonry
     smiles tingling in half-darkness
where serried shafts of light
filter through openings in massive walls

we climb spiralling steps
and gaze out from sun-struck terraces
onto dust and grazing for goats

     heat
     and silence

the squeak of a thorn tree bough

six a.m.

forty miles of rooftops
        flicker past the train window
under a chilly grey sky

        at Narita, boarding passes in hand:
        do we have time for coffee?

Garuda Indonesia regrets

        scaffolding encases
                the high rear engine of a DC-10
        mechanics toil
                under raised gull-wing cowlings

Flight 875 to Denpasar   indefinitely delayed

        passenger status:
                two small figures
        in the bottom left of an allegorical painting
        titled *The Penances of Air Travel*

*

meal trays come and go
Coltrane on the jazz channel
        comes round once an hour
the film projector breaks down

        (the myriad workings of this
        ramshackle tin bird lined with plastic)

at Jakarta
an hour and a half on the ground

covers raised on the left engine now
mechanics in oil-stained overalls
          crouch, peer with flashlights into
an interlocking three-dimensional jigsaw –
technology's bared blood vessels and veins

*

Denpasar, warm air at midnight,
          flowers beside the path
as we walk from tarmac to terminal

          insects dance in
          fuzzy arc light haloes

immigration, customs, taxi rank –
disarray, as at Manila or Bangkok, but here

          it's a gentle, undemanding polyphony

played out
          in a lilting minor key, and with
a scattering of petals and grace notes

THE WAVES

1 *Over the Mountains*

the minibus blares through
        a green world of palm tree
        banyan bamboo frangipani
swerves, horn blipping and braying, around
        ox carts parked jeeps
        stopped bemos skittering bikes
races below fields on steeply terraced hillsides
        (green rice yellow rice –
        two or three crops a year)
twists up into mountains
        (mosses shrubs trees and grasses
        banked green whorls of fern)
bowls northwards through the uplands
        (eastwards, blue volcanoes
        rise into pearly cloud)
descends to Singaraja
        (dim tree-lined streets slope
        gently through the town to the sea)
barrels along an avenue of ancient trees
        (broad whitewash sashes
        painted around their waists)
and drops us
at this palm- and bamboo-sheltered beach

...

bright painted outrigger canoes
        blue green blue yellow red
hauled up on the beach in a ragged line

failing light
slate-grey evening sea

cumulonimbus heaped
high on the horizon

    the day's last patch of blue
    streaked with wisps of cirrus

small waves
flop onto black volcanic sand

* * *

2 *In the Village*

a palm-fibre rope
    suspended from
        a line of planted sticks
leads out from the shore, supports

a net
whose upper edge is further buoyed
    by bobbing floats, made
from old cracked rubber sandals (everything is useful)

the fisherman
    sits all day
in a shady palm-frond shelter on the beach

wades out from time to time
        along the line
a triangular bamboo-framed scoop net in his hand

…

a man in a tattered straw hat
guides a heavy wooden plough drawn by two fat
brown oxen that
heave, them, selves, through

squelching, stubborn, thick, brown, mud

…

the lookout waits under his leafy roof

when a flock of birds
arrives to pillage the rice, he
agitates the web of threads
          that radiate from his shack
                  out across the fields, triggering a

     rattle and a clatter of
     dangling tin cans –

the flock explodes upwards and away

…

in paddy fields after planting
ducks feed all day on insects, snails and weeds

dabbling, paddling, aerating the water,
fertilising the fields with their droppings

until at sunset the duck-herds bring them
back along the beach to the village

fifty or sixty in each flock, all moving
as fast as their legs will carry them, necks

all thrust forward at the same intent angle
(a regiment of small fat men running through mud)

being 'driven' (although they know the way)
by a lad carrying

a wavering bamboo pole with a
white rag

lolling at the end of it

...

sunset:
huge cave of ragged fire

...

torrential rain in pitch darkness
      reverberant thunderclaps
rainwater pours from thatch
sheet lightning momentarily
         illuminates the rice paddies

    silhouetted palm trees
    gesticulate against the sky

dancing pencils of electricity
teeter on the jet-black sea

...

this temperate morning
        a man climbs a palm tree:
rope twisted in a figure of eight supports his feet
his hands grip the trunk
a machete is stuck in the belt of his shorts

the machete sounds
        high in the tree's bushy head
coconuts rain down, hit
the ground hard and heavy, and
bound across the grass

and then two or three
        brittle swathes of spiky leafage
crash down through the warm, still air, as
on the beach

the waves

make small lapping noises on the sand

PAK WAYAN, SITTING ON THE VERANDA
OF HIS LOSMEN

*we cannot afford politics, we must all work for
the country, for the growth of the country*

1965

*when we have developed the country, then maybe we
can have politics, but as for now
political parties are a danger, they divide the country*

80,000 dead in Bali alone

*but we debate, we take part in meetings, in
discussions, but they are always
to put a road in here, to dig a new well there*

murdered in villages, rice fields, ditches, lanes

*no politics, if you speak politics, they
will kill you just like that, I have seen it, and
it is right, no politics, first we must develop the country*

'small rivers and streams literally clogged with bodies'

SOME ROADS IN BALI

a quiet road below terraced paddy fields
a road dipping between earthen banks
a long, straight road lined with trees
three roads meeting in a patch of forest

a grassy track to a straggling village
a sandy lane towards the sound of ocean
a green-hedged defile
an open road downhill under an enormous sky

a road that climbs the volcano's shoulder
a potholed road between low buildings
a dark road lined with shuttered shops
a road that leads at night from village to silence

a full moon riding high above the trees

a tree-lined strip of tarmac threads
the life of the northern coast on its string

*every inch of the canvas should be filled, the figures embedded almost to
the point of disappearance among the frieze of leaf, plant and tree*

children burst out of houses by the roadside, hallo, hallo, big
grins, hands held out towards us (palms vertical, fingers splayed)

*let the painting be like the forest in all its anarchic orderliness, where
everything is decentred – or, if there are figures at or near the centre, a
maiden, for example*

laughing women carry sections of bamboo balanced on their
steady heads along a grassy path through trees

or a warrior

in the roadside barracks boys kneel to clip with shears the
commandant's lawn, young soldiers lounge with guns

*even then the detail of the rest of the painting should not be reduced to
'background' but should exist in its own prolific integrity*

dogs, chickens, ducks, grey piglets with spines so curved that
their bellies almost drag along the ground

*and the 'central' figure should be depicted merely as a figure that happens
to be in the middle of the canvas and not as any kind of centripetal or
radiating presence*

schoolboys in white shirts, names embroidered on their breast
pockets in blue, wait by the side of the road for the afternoon
bus home to their village

KUBUTAMBAHAN

1

steep steps ascend
      from a grassy terrace
to a stone platform with an empty throne

      (a sitting place for a god
      absent just now on heavenly business)

carved reliefs throng walls and balustrades:
flowers, tendrils, maidens, warriors, gods
      and mustachioed demons
with cavernous nostrils and apoplectic eyeballs

who lean towards us out of the stone
as yellow lichen grows quietly over their faces

2

back on the street
we sit on a wobbly roadside bench
beside a small shop selling
fruit, rice, baskets, bottles, sandals and soap

women chat, babies balanced on their hips
children squat to eat spiced soup
piglets forage among rickety food stalls
a dog sleeps in the dust

across the street a frangipani sheds
a petal or two into a stone-banked pond
half-choked with lilies and lotus plants
and sheeted with rich green scum

    the world is particular
    and perfect

a bus pulls up, a passenger
alights and offers
flowers
in a small palm-leaf tray at the temple gate

PURA BESAKIH

1

uphill on
foot a mile in the heat
the road points straight at the volcano

on either verge
        the slow spicy smoulder of
clove trees with red-tipped leaves

2

empty courtyards
        carved volcanic stone
raked gravel cross-hatched with
shadows of multi-storey thatched pagodas

beside stone steps
        a sheltered green hollow
the whisper of bamboo

3

17 *March* 1963

boulders, hot ash, mud flow, gravel
suffocating gasses, cinders, volcanic dust
villages incinerated and crops wiped out

lava within feet of its walls

4

boys sit on the gamelan pavilion veranda
rehearsing, getting it wrong, laughing, getting it right

MOUNT BATUR

Pine trees in mist, damp
jets of roadside fern, cloud-wrapped
houses with corrugated roofs along
an ancient volcano's rim – and then

the weather clears to reveal a caldera,
ten miles across, a grey-blue lake
curved against its inner flank, and an up-
thrust cindery cone rising at its centre

to three raw craters: ribbed mouths
stained with chemicals, fissures
in the habitable world of bamboo,
buffalo, rice plant, ant and egret,

where village women, serried
offerings of fruit and flowers
balanced on their heads, descend
with grace the path to the shrine,

past paddy fields stepping deftly down
a staircase of green terraces towards
the edge of the volcano's barren
boulder-strewn, outspread skirt

of ash and gravel, which twenty years ago
came fanning down – incandescent
and ungovernable – from the gaping
(and, just for now, quiescent) vents.

A DANCE IN UBUD

syntax of elbow and wrist
talkative fingers
punctuation by glance and raised eyebrow

knees flex,
exact swift placings of the feet
as though the dancer were

floating, were only deigning to
touch foot to floor
at the music's instigation

to humour it, to honour it
to point up its
effortlessly orchestrated syncopation

or as a favour to
the dignified seated musicians
whose mallets ding

on xylophones and gongs
(a consort of ringing treble
and groundswell bass),

who shift tempos without missing
a beat, their accents
jolting the staring wide-eyed dancer into

shiverings, abruptly poised stillness
and sudden
avalanches of gold-glittering movement

HALL OF JUSTICE

We gaze up at the painted ceiling
in the ultimate court of appeal
of the vanished kingdom of Klungkung –

the afterlife illustrated,
an encyclopaedia of the fates
awaiting unrepentant malefactors:

rape, dismemberment, attack by dogs,
assault with knives, clubs or spears,
ingestion by fiery-tongued dragons

or bisection of the skull
by dreadlocked demons wielding
double-handed saws with great élan.

BE GOOD OR LOOK WHAT YOU'LL GET!
is what the ceiling tries to say, but if
once it worked, it doesn't any more –

the artist spared no pains to represent
the last word in atrocity, but we today
can view his images almost with affection,

as marvellous naïveties, because
by now we know that hell is here
on earth and made by men, and is not

the visitation of any imaginable justice.

BOROBUDUR

I

an iron bridge across a torrential river
shanty shops beside the path
cold drinks and Buddha statuettes
baseball caps with peaks inscribed BOROBODUR

world mountain
        glimpsed through palm trees
a great beached vessel of grey volcanic stone

2

corridors thronging with carved reliefs
kings, queens, princes, courtiers
soldiers, servants, commoners, priests and hermits
cows, carts, ships, markets, temples, elephants
asuras, bodhisattvas, kinnaras, gandharvas and apsaras

    (the graceful tribhanga pose:
            flexed neck and hips,
        one leg relaxed, the other
                    supports the body's weight)

carved narratives of
the Buddha's previous incarnations
and his most recent life

nine clockwise spirals through the galleries
to reach the highest terrace

3

ranks of stone figures —
        the Buddhas of the four directions —
sit, gazing out over palm tree and rice field
to blue mountains wavering in distant haze

        on the fifth terrace, Vairochana,
        the Buddha of the zenith, instructs:

right palm raised and facing outwards
thumb and first finger joined in a circle

4

terrace after grey stone terrace,
a forest of iconography that has weathered
invasion, insurrection, the fall of kingdoms
earthquakes, eruptions, iconoclasts' hammers
tropical rains and the smother of jungle

designed by Gunadharma (ninth century)
using ratios of calendrical significance

        (the recent stone-by-stone restoration
        a seven-year, three-dimensional,
        two-hundred-thousand-ton jigsaw)

inhabited by no incarnate or commanding power
        a dance of carved stone above the abyss
        a mathematical flower of the void

5

the upper terraces are circular
no carvings
silent stone beneath blazing sun
an assembly of hollow bell-shaped stupas

diamond-shaped gaps in
latticework stone too hot to touch

    inside: Vajradhara
    the transcendent Buddha

hands poised in
circling dynamism, turning
the wheel of the law

6

A bus party of Muslim schoolgirls in the head-scarves
and long skirts of the Islamic revival laugh, chatter
and take photos of each other as they climb from level
to level: it's a fun day out. One lingers, then finds
herself separated from her companions. A small frown
troubles her face; she looks around and hesitates as if
perhaps hearing, just within earshot, a different music
from what she's used to being played.

(Many of the Buddha statues have been defaced – or
even decapitated – by iconoclasts.)

The other girls can be heard talking and laughing one level up. She stands, caught in this unexpected pause, small face framed by a coloured hijab, an anxious teen among the stone waves of iconography. Then she bethinks herself, and runs quickly up the steps to join her sisters.

7

at last the
uppermost stupa
on its lotus base

capped by a flat-topped
hexagonal spire
about 25 feet high

nothing inside it

empty and perfect

A COURTYARD IN BANGLI

ceramic tiles cool beneath bare feet

whitewashed walls

intermittent breeze

small flag on a bending rooftop pole

bamboo wind chimes dangle

random pentatonic notes

drop

from a deep blue sky

hear it

the invisible world of the wind

XIV

Habitat

from the top of Tokyo's highest building
on a clear day

7% of the world's GNP

The Real Thing

Aristotle Onassis's

barstools
upholstered in genuine

whale scrotum

Perestroika

bought these old battle tanks
from a new company over there in Leningrad

we have an option on a further 3,000 tons

it's good scrap metal
heavy and compact

Guinness Book of Records

Michael Milken
F. Ross Johnson
Charnoy Thipyasa

    $550 million
    $53.8 million
    141,078 years

        salary
        golden handshake
        imprisonment for fraud

Supper in Houston

140 cooks at work for four days

3 ½ tons of brisket, sausage, chicken, ribs
1 ½ tons of coleslaw, potato salad, beans
1,250 gallons of barbecue sauce, pickles, jalapenos
500 pounds of onions
5,000 servings of cobblers, carrot cake
650 gallons of lemonade, iced tea

six guests

a pair of ostrich boots, a 10-gallon hat, and a mandolin
for each
as a mark of the President's respect

Capitalism in the Eighties

we just couldn't
keep our hands off of it

The Albanian Deprivation

we're leaving our country
because we don't like the communists

we are young

we are poor

we've never even seen a
discotheque

Marketisation

in keeping with our commitment
to customer choice, you will pay
only for the air
you actually use

should you wish to exercise your right
not to breathe at all
there will be no charge other than
the meter rental fee

well Bob the spirit here seems to be very supportive certainly all the people I've spoken to both here and earlier in the day when I went out for a walk in the streets seemed pleased that Saddam is going to be taken down a notch and are very glad that finally this thing has at last got started and seem very elated by the early successes of the allied air power although of course this mood is to a certain extent fragile and we must remember that after the United States Egypt has the greatest deployment of troops in the theater that is about 40,000 in Saudi and another 5,000 in the Emirates and that there has been no ground action as yet and I think that once that ground action starts that if several thousand Egyptians are sent home in in in are sent home in er are sent home er

(dead)

I think that then the mood may change very rapidly and it would be difficult to maintain the initial enthusiasm and of course another factor is

17 *January* 1991

XV

IN THE WORLD

heaps of rubble
manholes without covers
open drains
uselessly set piles of cement

trishaws, tuk-tuks and buses
two-stroke engines and car horns
street vendors selling
bootleg cassettes and single cigarettes

warehouses shops and workshops
shutters raised
metal sheets and hanks of steel cable
bales bundles boxes crates and cartons

piles of planking and girders
disembowelled jeeps
the flash and sizzle of spot-welders
repair shops spilling out onto the street

air-conditioned banks guarded by
men in tight trousers, handcuffs
and truncheons adangle
from polished leather belts

as night falls, in every shack
the flickering light of the TV screen –
American heroes, Japanese anime,
or soft-spoken generals in spotless uniforms

speaking of duty, of family
of the safety of the nation –
a child plays in the dust
in the light that spills from the doorway

HOTEL BANGKOK

on the brightly lit sign in the street
        ringleted hair, a halo of flowers
        and the legend PARADISE FOR EVERYONE

in the ground-floor coffee shop
        young women in halter tops
        and fat pink men in shorts drinking beer

in the lobby
        backpackers
                (residua of a previous incarnation
                of this address as a travellers' junction)
        check their guide books

but all of these seem somehow less substantial than

        the miasmic reminders of the Founding,
        the wraiths of amphetamined GIs
        drifting in swathes along stark corridors
        seeking connection connection as you walk to your room

three layers in twenty years
an archaeology of atmospheres and economies

the key unlocks the door
        to a bare utilitarian room
with a message from The Management
stencilled on the mirror

        No Smoking In Bed

of which some previous occupant
assiduously with a razor blade
has scraped away the first five letters

GOLD RUSH

Mariposa, California

trail
camp
claim

tent city
saloon
whorehouse

murder a nightly occurrence

courthouse
jail
church

Indians negroes and mulattoes
may not testify against a white man
although they may testify against each other

town clock
hotel
railroad

closure of whorehouse

highway
Hollywood
chamber of commerce

TV

gifte shoppe

CEREMONY AT AYERS ROCK

1

the Anangu people
        prefer you not to climb it
they also don't call it that

        (some white premier of South Australia)

for them, climbing the rock
has but one fit occasion:
the opening of the men's initiation rites

        to ascend the sacred path
        to point a camera at the landscape?

the lens should be focused within

2

a thousand feet up on the bare red sandstone summit
a dawn wind shivering
across hundreds of miles of scratchy bush

snakes, wallabies, ghost gums, desert oaks
honey ants, lizards, spinifex, caterpillars, grubs

3

after the descent

walking in red dust below the massive sandstone shoulder
glimpse from a distance the initiation sites
partly masked by trees

no photographs please
even to stare is sacrilegious

4

the light plane heaves and slithers through
the furnace breath of desert updraughts,
crawls towards then circles high above Kata Tjuta

    huge lion paws of red conglomerate
    reposing in the pointillist bush

then turns and trembles back towards Uluru

I press the shutter button
(a new film loaded for this occasion)

    a click, an electronic whirr as
    the camera winds the unexposed film
    irretrievably back into its cassette

5

the plane lands
we unbuckle and clamber down the steps

after the climb has been completed
ensuing actions
whether dancing, walking or doing chores
are incorporated into the ritual and become sacred

dusty earth
walking barefoot, feel it hot between the toes

and this continues until the end of the ceremony

XVI

THE BURIAL MASK

behind the great eyes
behind the curving lips
behind the tangled locks embossed on the mask of gold

a void

      his children are statues
      his desires the beating of birds' wings
      the wind blows through the gaps between his thoughts
      his ships are anchored in a vanished harbour

the yellow stream brings down mud
and uprooted rushes – here
      where rain, wind and ruin meet,
the image of a face which grief has turned to stone

      we search in the shadow of the citadel
      we search by the long empty beach

the king
one word in Homer and that uncertain

do our fingers sometimes touch
his fingers' touch upon the stones?

LOVE'S LABOUR

I

he arrives then
unexpected, bewildering
black-cloaked and mud-bespattered

    I bring you news

to dance a galliard is an artifice
    a witty thing to do with your feet
but not necessarily on that account to be avoided
the peacock spreads its feathers in courtship

    but that thou interrupt'st our merriment

I bring news of mortality to your revels
I bring sombreness, necessity
    and new authenticities to test your love
I bring the cuckoo and the owl
    the pageant of the seasons
above all I bring orders for the braggart soldier:
to till the earth for his love

worthies away, the scene begins to cloud

    a twelvemonth and a day
    that's too long for a play

2

ancient figures
eyes glittering behind their masks

tree with its roots sunk deep in mumming

    a masque of the seasons, how
    could we make one,
    how could we shape one now?

rubbish heap and filthied nest
massacre by proxy sneaking through the greenwood
invisible inquisition
meddlesome meddling fingers

    Homo indignus
    strolls in the garden of his entitlement

nevertheless
this moment of an old communion

    the courtiers to-wit to-woo

real owls answer from the dusk

3

our wooing doth not end like an old play
Jack hath not Jill

     you that way, we this way

frosts and fasts
hard lodging and thin weeds

to move wild laughter in the throat of death

     that a jest's prosperity
     lies in the ear of him that hears it, never
     in the tongue of him that makes it

to learn this, to prove it, to live it

the cycle of the seasons
the twelve celestial signs
     all these are well beyond our control

she's quick, she's two months on her way
the child brags in her belly
she lies back against the trunk of the tree
under autumnal boughs in evening light

a child of our Grandmother Eve
a female
or for thy more sweet understanding a woman

and her smile rims the centuries with desire

SIX

(1991–2002)

XVII

TO WHOM IT MAY CONCERN

I imagine you reading this.

You must be reading now, since if you're not, these sentences don't exist. So: if you find yourself reading them, you can be sure that so far, up to and including this moment, everything must be all right.

Tonight the stars glitter frostily in the sky above Tokyo, and the ducks are upending themselves in the dark, feeding in the cold and flowing river.

The next sentence was supposed to begin with *we* – but who is that? You and me, obviously; many others, some of whom may not yet be born as I write; probably not the ducks – and perhaps not even me – by the time you read this; certainly not all of those who were alive when a few moments ago I wrote the sentence about stars and sky and ducks and river. And absolutely not the stars; they glitter frostily, and can never be included.

But at any rate, the *we* is a temporary one, a fellowship that includes, you can be sure, at least you, together with some others known to you, who I cannot imagine, but to whom I, as your companion in this moment of language, send my greetings.

And what I want to say is that stars glitter frostily above a cold and flowing river; that ducks upend themselves in the dark to feed; and that we (I send my greetings) are here for a little longer yet and

that is a shareable joy.

With bread, of course, it's hopeless: slice after slice disappearing into consumption's maw.

Cake, crust and crumb – all vanish into the void of a hunger of which they can have no conception. What's left of the dear departed pizza? A cardboard coffin, a rumour of tomatoes, a belch's brief memorial.

But nobody wants to eat shoes. They, surely, should outlast their bony occupants, if not the pavements that grant them their daily friction.

Only one or two outings, though, and already they're old and daft; a few days more and they're infecting the whole wardrobe with the sorrows of the uninhabited.

Any moment now we'll see them, laces dangling, tongues flapping in inaudible protest, as they're shuffled off into the furnace's mouth.

TROUSERS

'All that damned buttoning and unbuttoning,' said the demented aristocrat just before he killed himself.

Braid, medals, ribbons, linen – the froth upon the thing itself. I am a plucked fruit shrivelling inside my tailor's instructions.

The best we can do: the forked radish and noble cabbage up to their knees in dirt; the mad king in his nightshirt trying to instruct the Atlantic.

Man is born naked, and everywhere he is in trousers.

The city's boast: what's done is done.

But this is empty talk. What's really happened is that land has suffered bricks to set up camp.

The eyes trace contours, the ripple of hills and valleys beneath the urban grid; the nostrils drink the wind of once-and-future heath and holt.

1. Honey. Apples. Summer in an orchard. A treatise on gardens.

2. A grey wolf is observed among the hollyhocks. The donning of a mask. Manifold complications and a misplaced key.

3. Thunder. Catastrophe. Tempests and earthquakes. An old man jumps from a very high bridge.

4. Multiplying disguises. Scenes of unbridled lust. The gaoler with a rubber nose. The beautiful animal is tormented in its golden cage. Seventeen rapes, five eviscerations, and the destruction of several large cities.

5. Providential manipulations and rearrangements. Thoughts on fatherhood. Three unlikely marriages and a humble restitution. After a short pause for refreshments, the whole thing starts all over again.

UTOPIA, ARCADIA

The 3:19 passes through a cutting and across a matchstick bridge above a glassy river. It's running right on time. It continues through a level crossing and comes to a halt in a station equipped with bookstall, milk churns and a motionless porter.

The man watches over his creation, his hands resting lightly on the controls. He likes to wear a uniform while he plays.

In the station yard a little figure is lifting a bale into a warehouse beneath the light bulb sun. Never let it be thought that this figure might be unhappy – he likes to do what he's supposed to do. This is Utopia, every detail perfect.

2

In a circle of lamplight a man raises his eyes from a page. The poems he's been reading have led him, step by step, to a small clearing in the forest of his perplexity.

They're a hint and a reminder, telling him of a world in which the annals of atrocity aren't opened from one year to the next. If you go to the central archive of Arcadia and ask the librarian for guidance, he'll scratch his head; even he doesn't know where such chronicles are shelved.

A train passes in the night, its sound coming through the forest and across small lakes and meadows. In the villages and market towns along its route the windows rattle in their frames and children stir in their sleep.

Once a month they come to this room with its bar, crowded tables and bandstand, and here they do what they like to do. Three saxophones, two trumpets and one trombone, piano, guitar, bass and drums – together they make one complex, syncopating voice. Breathe in concert: voice the line: convert black dots into transient sculptures of air. Ten players, and not a finger out of place.

The trombonist stands to take his solo. Microsecond by microsecond, with fluid wrist and accurate lip, he alters the air pressure in the room. Plump, delicious triplets, runs of bitter-sweet semiquavers.

The band is right there behind him: the gentle bass player, who likes to listen to wood; the guitarist, who plots chords on his fingerboard and will never tell you how he feels; the drummer, who pushes time forward with sticks and brushes; the pianist, connoisseur of the displaced arpeggio and altered chord; and the brass and saxes, breathing a sinuous melodic line which then they harmonise and weave into a tapestry of voicings.

Patterned nerves, crafted embouchure, fingers' adept touch: every player who ever lived has had a different sound, and the one most final word for death is silence. Breathe together: voice the line: make a good sound in this fugitive space. Time is not clocks but breath, and this is the game we love to play with ears and air.

And then people began to keep pet rocks. The rocks came in different sizes; people gave them names and dressed them in ribbons and leather collars and carried them out to the garden so they could have a look at the world each day.

This didn't escape the attention of the cats, who left. Every one of them. No, I tell a lie, there was an elderly tabby living in one of the outer suburbs of Vienna who stayed, but he was crazy and mangy and not long for this world.

The feline exodus made quite an impact. Canaries and budgerigars fell silent in their cages. Dogs sat in dark places with furrowed brows. Hamsters, gerbils and white mice stopped running in their treadmills and sat motionless in the sawdust, gazing out between the bars.

I come back to the hotel but find it's under new management. There's the same tatty red carpet in the corridor, but both walls have been lined with mirrors. It's disconcerting to walk between them, to be plunged into this mise en abyme. What am I supposed to do about boundaries?

The new owner is sitting in one of the bedrooms drinking tea. I point out that some of his guests may have trouble dealing with the multiplying reflections, especially where the corridor is wide and the mirroring walls are too far apart to touch.

'Infinity is difficult,' I say.

'You mean because it's cold?' he asks.

XVIII

IN ARLES

1

an avenue of Roman sarcophagi
stone fragments shaded by rustles and whispers
pine trees, oak trees
          green voices sprouting from a midden
of dislodged columns and broken white stones

a Jesuit chapel, its walls
encrusted with the scabs and sores of Baroque,
          its altars like fetishists' masks –
a stone pestilence with its foundations plunged deep
in an underworld of Roman storerooms,
musty vaults where dampness drips on gravel
and footfalls mutter among shadows and silences

and near the river a tumble of brick
the residue of a world
          of nacreous mists and bathhouse sensualities
stripped now of its skin of tile and marble
a heap of pink rubble under the arch of the sky

(step through a hole in a wall
find nothing
but an absence at the heart of desire)

2

the curve of the arena crests the town
with its arches of crumbling grey stone

the death of yesterday's bull is a stain on the sand
and today the sunlight
          and the high silent air of the terraces
still throb with the roar of the vanished crowd

an echo of an echo: beneath the arena
in dark passageways, whose earthen floors
          are pungent with the taint of stale urine,
older and more brutal ghosts
condense out of vapour in the stone-cooled air

raucous with festival
          they climb worn steps to high-banked seats
to watch animals, misfits, and professional murderers
being rendered to gobbets and nothingness

and it makes them drunk
these voyeurs
they are stirred as they flirt with oblivion

(by their desire shall you know them
they paint their hunger on empty air)

3

gravel paths, municipal benches
pine trees, plane trees loud with cicadas

a madman strides through the park
          scattering the sparrows and pigeons,
jerking and flaring
as jolts of aberrant energy pulse through his frame

a Second Empire fountain
spouts cold torrents from its cast-iron mouth
onto a cluster of carved nymphs miming abandon

mnemic traces
desire stiffened to marble
and draped with a fig leaf of classical reference

4

roots entangled in the wreckage of empires
cellars crammed with cruelties and disaster
the detritus of history is built into our own domestic walls

    opportunists, jackdaws
    connoisseurs of expedient rubble
    we will make our nests out of anything

the ghosts have followed from the arena
eddying and swirling, darkening the sunlight

turbulent voices
    eruption of banished deprivations
they have come on a journey of two thousand years
to poison the house of the present

you filch from the past, they say
to house your own purpose, which is
to elide the unbearable
and conjure pain to forgetfulness

your life is a house of denials
your foundations are sunk in a chosen oblivion
but there's no escape from the past
nor from the impulses that made it

how to dispel these ghosts?
perhaps perfect stillness can do it

    limit the damage
    imagine a windless night
    turn the wick down to a bud of flame
    shelter its frailty from all intrusion

we are wild weather, the ghosts say
cupped hands are no defence against our gales

5

corroding sheet metal
rasping scurf of polystyrene
junked air conditioners bleeding their chemicals

in a weed-grown lot
the corpse of a Lambretta bares its bones

rusting ganglia and rotting tyres
curved fenders
a Venus of the age of technology
recumbent in the heat and silence of noon

6

the great curve of the Rhône is ruffled with eddies

Alpine snowmelt, run-off from foothills,
a braided muscle of currents
flexing between embankments of close-set stone

evening
and people step out into late sunlight
        hospitable to whatever encounters
might saunter towards them on cooling pavements,
heading for cafés, bars, or the houses of friends
so the unexpected may disclose itself and be greeted
so they may go on undaunted
        shaping their lives in the river of moments
in which they are shaped by each moment

the ghosts say:

why did you summon us anyway?
it was your own hunger you spoke of
you only needed us
to tell yourself what you've done with your life

but we are the past, we were different
and your life has its own occasions
its own course through salt marsh and circumstance
to an estuary's unravellings

we have power only if you give it to us
we can't harm you unless you choose to be harmed

there is a comfort in contingency
in making our lives
from gifts our hunger could never elicit

the ghosts disperse into cool evening air

bats shuttle, flit in the twilight, swerve past
        flaked inscriptions on the arena's walls
where beady-eyed pigeons
roost in pairs in the masonry's fissures

trees by the tombs stir and whisper,
adding rings of cells to their girth
as their roots sift the mulch of centuries

above the open-air cafés in the Place du Forum
the sky fades from turquoise to aubergine
        then deepens to Indian ink
and the square is a murmur of voices
into which a nightingale spills song from a plane tree
a thread of melody embroidering the talk and laughter

which one traveller alone with his glass of wine
takes as a promise that
in the unrepetitive dapple of incompletion
his hunger will be fed with something other than hunger

XIX

MIDWINTER

I

I thought the night would never end
although actually, of course, it was day

borne up on the long
        wavering tremble of riveted wings
through twelve hours of Siberian darkness
seat belts fastened and headphones on

        Hollywood hallucinations
        flickering on the bulkheads –

            car chase and shoot-out
            explosion after explosion
            Bruce Willis covered in blood –

 as we burrow through the Arctic night
        two hundred strangers
in a temporary projectile village

trailing behind us
the thin dispersing plume of our exhaust

2

Copenhagen at midnight,
dark water, and a snowy canal-side path
to a hotel room where on the multichannel
the dreaming goes on and on:

Tannenbaum and fir trees from Germany,
    rock music videos from London,
a nervy Swedish costume drama with a yule log,
    five glum Norwegians singing folk songs,
and, to a blare of car horns, the descent on wires
    of Santa Claus into a floodlit Italian piazza

I press the remote at random
and stumble into radio, where
        in a sudden hush, Stan Getz
is playing 'Softly, As In a Morning Sunrise'

March 1991, Café Montmartre
        just down the road from here
his next-to-last gig and his last recording

faultless – variation after variation,
embouchure strong and
        steady despite the cancer,
his luminous, misty-but-edged-with-steel tone
unillusioned in the midwinter dark

3

towards dawn I dream I have a new apartment,
painted white,
bookshelves and furniture not yet installed

but an inhabitable space,
and one whose after-waking flavour lingers –

       a savour of new beginnings, as tentative as
       a convalescence, as equivocal

as that long grey line on the horizon
visible from the taxi during
the dawn trip back to the airport

which might be Sweden seen across the Øresund
in early morning light
or might just be
         a low grey shelf of mist
                  suspended
in cold midwinter haze between sea and sky

Tokyo–Copenhagen, 23–24 December 1995

ON ARRIVAL

The steel guard rail chills the fingers
as the vaporetto feels its way in mist
along the Grand Canal. The pulse

of the engine echoes back from dark
palazzi, changing key as we approach
each stop, where the boatman loops

twin steel bollards with a nonchalant
figure of eight of hairy yellow rope,
which squeaks and groans as it takes

the strain – until, in the swirl and wash
of arrival, the vessel warps into exact
alignment with the jetty, so we may step

from the shift and sway of the deck
to the pontoon's sway and shift
and onto the fondamenta's stone.

Venice, 24 December 1995

ACQUA ALTA

1

the top of the Campanile is lost in mist,
in a hush of drizzle and darkness

and then the bells begin to sound, first
one bell, then another and another

reverberations tumbling from the sky
to flood the square

with all the force and weight
of Venice before it became a jewel-box

not bells as harmony, not
a simulacrum of the music of the spheres

but something visceral, an insistence
that penetrates the bones –

we stand in the dark piazza
inhabited by bells

2

and then they stop

one by one
they swing themselves back to silence
and the air falls still again

darkness
a prickle of drizzle on upturned faces

a quietness in which we can hear
a ripple of voices and
the small lapping of footfalls on stone

Venice, 24 December 1995

MIRACLES

> *Giovanni Bellini: Polyptych of St Vincent Ferrer*

nine panels
encased in intricate gold

on the base
       three small scenes depict
St Vincent performing miracles, bringing
succour to the faithful in their hour of need:

swooping out of the sky
on a saint-sized magic carpet of fluffy cumulus
to free the prisoners and raise the dead

arriving in a puff of smoke
his arms outstretched
       his halo undisturbed by flight
to guide the rescuers to a buried child
in the rubble of an earthquake-ruined city

hovering solicitously over
a drowned but about-to-be-resurrected woman
       a sodden white bundle half-submerged
in a glinting rippling tide race,
in water which is pure vision of water

       a liquid hallucination
       brimming between earthen banks

water on earth as it is in heaven
shining and purling before my faithless eyes

Venice, 28 December 1995

LA SERENISSIMA

for Dorsey and Sandra

1

dark alleys
stone pavements beside misty sage-green canals

damp crumbling brick
damp marble
damp limestone

the long low line of San Michele
arched water gates
and red-brick walls fledged with cypresses
suspended between grey-green sea and dove-grey sky

rain beats on the vaporetto windows
the boat judders against the landing stage
waves splash up over worn steps of Istrian stone

2

rain hisses on the canal beneath our windows
and along the calle a shutter bangs all night in an empty tenement
as the storm comes unimpeded out of the Adriatic
pulsing in across the Lido beneath a sky of dark driven clouds

a century and a half ago, the Austrians
moored this city to the mainland with a causeway
but Venice tonight is out at sea among the elements
wind, sweeping rain and scudding clouds

at dawn
salt squalls whip the lagoon to curds of froth

3

late afternoon and the sun breaks through
rainwater glistens on canal-side paving stones
the sky still full of intimations of future weather
the Canale della Giudecca the colour of green tea

and then for ten minutes
the Basilica's cowled tympana all blaze with gold

until the light fades, the moment passes
and soon, seen from the Piazzetta,
the day expires in tattered pinks and vermilions
behind the domed silhouette of Santa Maria della Salute

4

the next day to Torcello across choppy green seas
following the lines of bricole
steel bands hooping the clustered pilings
some surmounted by a faintly glowing beacon
or topped with a seagull or two

past abandoned islands –
broken-backed jetties, tumbled sea walls
red-brick ruins, foreshores of mud –

and then at reduced throttle through the canal at Mazzorbo
wake mounting and falling away from stone-faced banks

and out to a loneliness of marsh and low horizons
reed beds ruffled by eddies of skittering wind
small water birds upending themselves, flipping out of sight
for whole minutes beneath the surface
and then reappearing just where you least expect them

5

at Torcello a big sky
a wire-mesh fence
and small cold comments from the wind

a brick-paved path beside a small canal
from landing stage to basilica
fields and tamarisks brown with winter
and at each stage of the walk, on wall-top or gatepost,
a different cat waiting plumply to be stroked and petted

and inside the cathedral
cool grey-green light and mosaics glowing with gold

at the east end Madonna and child
lean down from the curve of the vaulting
at the west end a *Last Judgement* thronged with the damned,
Byzantine heads afloat in a sea of flames
while the saints stand in clusters looking up to their Redeemer

each face different but all rhyming
in the formality of their act of attention

6

and today a last vaporetto

an extended trance on grey-green water under an eggshell sky
up the avenue of palazzi knee-deep in winter
red brick, patterned brick and marble
water slapping at walls and flaked wooden doors

all the way from San Marco
to the windy vault of Santa Lucia
where the trains stand under the canopy
resting their dead weight on grimy steel springs in the shadows

7

but what I most want to remember
although I cannot properly
is the Basilica

the clustering domes
the groves of marble and porphyry pillars
the roofline a breaking wave of stone foliage, of saints and angels
the glow of mosaic above doorways
the horses of Byzantium flaring on the terrace

accretion and incrustation
addition and growth
design filling out, ornamentation finding its place

a building which grew like a seashell or like coral
and now is too various, and much too in love with detail
to be reduced to a single image

Venice & after, 29 December 1995

DUOMO

for Sandra

we pause on a ledge high above
        the patterned marble of the cathedral floor
to watch the *Last Judgement* of Vasari and Zuccari –
        a wrestling match of saints and angels
        trumpeted in a hundred colours –
swarm out of the painted firmament just above our heads

then duck under a stone lintel
from this narrow, vertiginous walkway
        into a spiral staircase, a corkscrew
of claustrophobia, which worms its way up inside
the massive fabric of the dome

look! cracks in the masonry, blocks
forced out of alignment, or even split in two,
iron staples holding things in place –

what if it all came down?

        a huge collapsing rumble, thousands of tons
        of disintegrating brick and marble,
        flailing angels, tourists in their raincoats,
        God Almighty himself entangled in the fabric
        as it all goes down in a Niagara of dust and plaster

best not think about that, best go on
step by step
up and up and up and finally out
onto a marble balcony under a weathering sky:

a whole city down there, swept by rain

Florence, 30 December 1995

PALAZZO PITTI

an uphill sweep of piazza to
an intimidating cliff of rusticated stone

inside, too, you're meant to be daunted –
the stone staircase much too wide
the apartments far too grand
the furnishings and art too high and mighty

> *frescoes, mouldings, tapestries*
> *gold, ormolu, satin, damask*
> *chinoiserie, chandeliers*
> *marble-inlay tables by the gross*

back outside, the sky darkens and turns to downpour:
rain cascades from stone eaves, spouts
from lead pipes and gutters
into the Medicis' courtyard

we scuttle downhill through the cloudburst
to a café where
we dry out among these others
whose shoes, skirts and trouser legs are also soaked

companionable strangers
with whom we share the world and its weather

Florence, 31 December 1995

AT FIESOLE

I

three hours on foot to Fiesole

steep lanes between mossy walls
villas sheathed in tangling ivy
cypresses flexing in the wind

then high above the valley
a paved terrace to walk about on
a platform with a lip of stone, where

you can lean out over a parapet and see
the world below
with the Duomo in the middle of it

go on a few more steps to the Franciscan friary
a herb garden
a cloister and a row of cells

each cell six feet by six
with plank bed
and shelf and desk and chair and book

a place you could live for ever and day by day
breathe emptiness to incarnation
drawing up vision like water from a well

2

in the chapel an *Adoration of the Magi*

descending a dusty road through the Tuscan landscape
among donkeys and oxen, pilgrims, peasants and shepherds
keeping good company
making its way to the manger

a small giraffe steps delicately
come all the way from Africa
with dappled hide, knobbly knees and an innocent exalted stare

3

the world tingles in its particularity

in a bare room
the sky has been bound between black covers
and chained to a desk

a novice looks up from the page
then closes the book

and steps out
into an ordinary astonishing universe
just beyond everything he'd thought of as God

Fiesole, 1 January 1996

FONTE GAIA

1

in the cathedral museum in Siena, Duccio
has a small room to himself

where a line of chairs is drawn up
        in front of *The Madonna Enthroned*
as if in a theatre, so you can sit and watch
the assembled ranks of bearded saints and dreaming angels
performing stillness

        and listen in the silence to
        their golden haloes chime

like very gently struck gongs

2

in the sloping piazza, beneath
a curved façade of red mediaeval brick

        Fonte Gaia, the 'joyous fountain'

where pigeons flutter, ruffle and perch
        on the heads and laps of sculpted Virtues,
bathe in the fountain's splash and tingle,
spreading their wings in the threads of water
that spout from the mouths of marble wolves

a puppy
lollops around all this in an ecstasy of exploration
Young Master Hound
trot and sniff, bounce and bark

nose down
start back sideways in surprise
such rich, such unpredicted smells
how extraordinary to have a tail and shadow

3

in a panel on the Baptistry ceiling
a *Day of Judgement*

large stars
evenly spaced in a deep blue sky
where red-faced angels blow their trumpets

an ochre desert
out of which the dead are resurrecting

one head after another
breaking through the earthy crust
up and out from blankness into unexpected air

Siena, 2–3 January 1996

THE VISIT

in memory of Jo Sawbridge (1945–70)

when she visited tonight
she was cheerful and friendly
as young as ever
and happier than I'd seen her for years

but even in my dream I knew she was dead

I get up and cross the room
open the shutters, look down
at lines of parked cars, street lamps
wet tarmac, running gutters

    twenty-six years

the dead do come back
but then again, of course, they don't

Milan, 5 January 1996

MIDWINTER RETURN

I

Copenhagen
    snow and darkness

the plane has been pushed back from the gate
and pauses on the apron, where
two squat mechanical arachnids
    heads ablaze with floodlights
come to cure our frozen skin of ice,
reaching out with nozzled limbs to blast
    their scouring juices onto fuselage and wings
while the plane submits, trembling
from tail to nose beneath the impact

    a midwinter shamanistic techno-rite

then the plane begins to move again,
shivers and wobbles laboriously towards the runway
its belly full of clicks and whines and buzzes

another pause, and then
    the whole huge weight
of riveted metals, moulded plastics
fuel pipes, electronic ganglia and tons of kerosene

launches itself along the concrete
lifting off at last
at full throttle into the northern night

2

dawn
the flaps unsheathe in sections
        from the trailing edges of the wings
are adjusted and readjusted
as the plane begins its bumpy descent

        wrinkled coastline, coruscating sea
        patchwork rice paddies
        groves of bamboo, green knolls of pine
        plastic greenhouses, small farms and country roads

and then the wheels go down
and we come skimming in above a line of beacons
        (the bow wave's surge as we follow the line of bricole)
to meet the runway with a jolt
        (the horses of Byzantium proudly pawing the ground)

tyres smearing concrete
with streaks of burnt rubber in early morning light

Copenhagen–Tokyo, 5–6 January 1996

XX

BRANCH LINE

1

embankments bake
        beneath a blanket of summer grasses
heat haze wavers above shimmering rails

flaked wooden sleepers
        blackened with spilt diesel
sunk deep in a stained brown bed of crunching ballast
each as big as a man and as heavy

the whole of life is a bruise
a memory of the locomotive's trampling tons

2

the train which arrives is not a fancy train

no plastic
no discreet hiss of the automatic
no carriage doors breathing themselves open and shut

get on and the door swings shut behind you
with a double clunk redolent of the decades

grey windows
stained with the dribbles of ancient rainstorms
a hot whiff of faded upholstery
a litter of tabloids and crushed cigarettes

a bucking rattling journey
on a line that goes off at a tangent through derelict places

scorched cuttings and sudden dark tunnels
crumbling Victorian viaducts
boarded-up warehouses on hot dusty streets

3

travelling laterally
through the marginal boroughs
deaf to the call of the big destinations

begin to notice
back gardens patched
with bright-coloured laundry

allotments stitched
with neat rows of green

the weeds flower
in vacant lots

purple and yellow and blue

> *the weather of course never comes*
> *from the quarter one has been carefully observing*
> (Sigmund Freud to Sandor Ferenczi)

the river is talking in its sleep
as it flows beneath the big deaf trees

in the heart of its transparent heart
it remembers itself
issuing cleanly from a cleft in the rock

but now it feels like a changeling
soiled and unstanchable
muttering and shivering in its muddy bed

    I want to stop dead in my tracks
    I want time to work things out
    I want to know when I first made my mind up
    I want someone to explain the joke

    I want to give myself elocution lessons
    I want to know where rain comes from
    I want to know if there's any truth
    in the rumours I've heard of the sea

so much to know, so much to judge and master –
but deep in the swim of itself
it knows it will never be the world's greatest expert

on hydraulics or hydrography
or hydrology or hydromancy
or hydromania or hydrotherapy or even hydronymy

and daily it reinvents itself
in spite of its most earnest intentions
in the slaps and slops which slip from its liquid tongue

in inundations and *divertissements*
in cascades and escapades
and idles that would never have entered its head

ONE WAY

there are a lot of ways to feel terrible

that woman in her crumpled blue raincoat
in the coffee shop
eyes closed, hands clasped, lips moving in prayer

until she gives it up
half-opens her eyes to take
a sip of coffee
as though it were a bitter medicine

and lights a cigarette
not noticing
her last one still burning in the ashtray

FOR PESSOA

Fernando
>   whose heart was an overturned bucket

Fernando
>   who waited patiently for them to open a door
>   at the foot of a wall in which there was no door

Fernando
>   who sang the ballad of the infinite in a chicken-coop
>   and heard the voice of God in a well with a lid

have you got over your terrible cold
>   your chill that made even metaphysics sneeze?

have you finished your apprenticeship in unlearning?
>   are you cured at last of being cured?

the beasts graze on green grass not knowing their names

the wind forgets the shapes of its grief

you bend your head over the river of the page
a sign hung on your door which says *Gone reading*
how can I know you in your knowing?
wade in deep to cast for stippled trout
swim naked against the current's cool persistent pull
dream all afternoon on the whispering riverbank
brimming water
never the same text twice

CONCERTO PICCOLO

(for the players of the Vienna Art Orchestra)

flumpelhorns and euboniums
claxinets and fluxophones

paeanoforte
scattervox
and double bello

alpenhum
marimbelanophone
and plethoral drumcussions

EISENSTADT

in a park
behind a palace where Haydn used to play,

a grey lake agitated by a chilly wind
        a rotunda on a rocky knoll
and big old trees not responding yet to spring

the winter-shuttered orangery,
        where string quartets will perform
for townsfolk and tourists on balmy summer nights,
hibernates in its own silence
on a broad gravel terrace fringed with balustrade

in town the main street is neat and clean
beneath the pale sun of early spring

cream and yellow eighteenth-century houses
a Renaissance town hall with frescoes of the Virtues
citizens in overcoats
parking cars and going in and out of shops

in the Jewish cemetery
the headstones lean at angles in thick green grass

THE PAINTING STICK

Flying over the Crimea in 1943, *his Stuka plane was shot down by Russian anti-aircraft fire. While lying in a twenty-day coma in hospital, he imagined his rescue by a tribe of Tartars who wrapped him in fat and felt to keep him warm.*

I

a hunter crouches
deep in a cave in the Upper Palaeolithic

in flickering tallow light
with stone palette
      and earth pigments at hand
he gazes at the contours of the limestone wall

in the daylight world
      out on the windy steppe
the animals have slipped in under his guard
untamed presences muscled with light

and now in this fissure
      he can see them
in the curves and bulges of water-formed rock

he picks up his painting stick:
living deer leap out of the rock face to meet him

      fifteen thousand years

the steel door of the Grotte de Font-de-Gaume
booms as it closes behind us
      and our eyes adjust to the darkness:

mammoths
        aurochs and fine-limbed horses
  in brown haematite and black manganese

fleet deer
the brown-shouldered bulk of bison

2

hours spent by a child

faces or landscapes
in the wallpaper
in tumbled blankets on the bed
in damp stains on walls, on floors
in lichen on rocks
in the coal fire's hot crevices
in summer's slow clouds unfurling against the blue

living presences
envisioned out of whatever is offered

dreaming wide-eyed as he follows the contours
absorbed in the world's fluid grammar of hints

3

in the forecourt of the Royal Academy
Sir Joshua Reynolds poses with palette and brush
a balletic gesture stiffened to bronze

the voice of Blake
        fulminating in Lambeth
carries from across the river, from across the centuries
and echoes faintly in the courtyard

        folly! of what consequence is it to the arts
        what a Portrait Painter does?

we ascend in a steel-and-glass lift to the galleries
and enter the cave of Beuys

pencil, wax, watercolour, hare's blood, fat

deer, goats, bees, a volcano, a glacier
and nameless shapes in red and brown and ochre

drawing as dreamwork with pencil in hand
a daily record
        vestiges, traces of inhabitation
discovering forms to think with on paper
as the contours of the moment suggest them

no 'technique'
        but that's part of the point

why is this as comforting as it is?

        shaman for a murderous century

a man trapped in a plane
as it plunges towards the earth in flames

born in the year of Servesterpool
North Corner, Devenport, Russian War

Odyssean voyagings
a pony cart clopping through the streets of St Ives
townful of shallows, gulls on the sailing roofs

   rag-a-bone! old iron!
   A. Wallis, Dealer in Marine Stores

death of Mrs Susan Wallis, formerly Mrs Susan Ward
(£8 15s for making a Pitchpine Coffin)
after which he began to paint (with ship's paints) ships
on cardboard got from Mr Baughan the grocer
Duty Mighty and the Devil in the upstairs room

Knocked Down by a Moter Car in The Street
Molisted in the High Rod Cigven hill

looks as though Mr Wallis is goin to have one o they bad turns

two loaves of bread a week, 5d
allus ad is trousers too big, e didn care, rolled the buggers up
filth, fleas and senile dementia
voices coming down the chimney
damn Catholic! Methodist! Irishman! thief!
death in penury in Madron workhouse

I paint things what used to be
and there is only one or two what has them
and I does no harm to anyone

ALFRED WALLIS

ARTIST & MARINER

1855 aug 19   aug 29 1942

INTO THY HANDS O LORD

his past house hung in foreign galleries
the gulls wade into silence

VENETIAN CASTLE: IRAKLION

I

a squat gateway flanked by cannon ports
the cobbled darkness of the magazine

sun-struck battlements from which
steel-clad sentries scanned the sea lanes

the winged lion hunkers on its plaque
claws unsheathed on open book
attentive still
to what *la Serenissima* was built on –

the firepower of the vanished guns,
the logged forests of Veneto
                              pile-driven
deep into other people's histories to sustain

that frieze of palaces and bell towers
shimmering at dawn between lagoon and sky

       no such beauty here

empire is empire
a knuckle of intimidating stone

2

it ended in ruin
after a twenty-two year siege:

the state of the town
was terrible to behold, the streets
were covered with bullets and cannonballs
and shrapnel from mines and grenades

there was not a church,
not a building even, whose walls
were not holed and almost
reduced to rubble by the enemy cannon

everywhere the stench was
nauseating, at every turn
one came upon
the dead, the wounded or the maimed

3

a placid working harbour now

fishing smacks cluttered with tackle
rusting bollards
nets spread out to dry

seventy miles away
pennants flutter at the mastheads
of the sleek grey warships
leashed to their moorings in Souda Bay

KNOSSOS

ruins are hard to read:
how to imagine a world
from the bottom six inches of a storehouse wall?

        fat red and black pillars,
        ferroconcrete, pastel-coloured murals –
        a ruin fabricated, it seems,
        in the early nineteen-hundreds

what if Sir Arthur had just bared the stones,
no more mediation than that,
would Minoan ghosts appear more readily?

        outside the wire-mesh fence
        air-conditioned buses stand in a shimmer of heat
        inside, queues
        move slowly through reconstructed rooms

a woman waits with camera poised
        in front of a fresco of a prancing bull
for a shot with no passers-by

her image
of having been here all alone with history

ARKADI

Corinthian columns, baroque lintels
double belfry, double nave,
        a sandstone cloister with
battlements running the length of its roof –

in the museum, sepia photographs
(bandoliers, sheepskin boots and fierce moustaches)
        and a large-scale map with arrows
showing the Turkish advance across the hills –

an explosively opened vault, once the magazine,
where, when the Turks broke in at last,
        the abbot set off the powder
killing hundreds, Greeks and Turks alike –

outside, across the dusty car park,
a small domed building containing only
        – as eyes adjust to the darkness –
a glass-fronted cabinet full of human skulls

PAN

after Angelos Sikelianos

rocks on a deserted shore
where noon shimmers
above burning pebbles and emerald waves

Salamis a blue trireme out at sea
the pines and mastic trees of Kineta a deep breath in the lungs

a flock of iron-grey goats clatters headlong down the hill

fingers pressed against his tongue
the goatherd
with two harsh whistles huddles them together on the shore

they settle among the brush and wild thyme
goatherd and goats
dozing in the silence of noon

a goat gets to its feet
moves alone towards a rock which juts into the sea

and stands there
motionless
at the very edge where the spray dissolves

upper lip pulled back so that his teeth shine
smelling the white-crested sea until sunset

ANTIQUITIES

how sad the museums are

who wore these earrings?
who placed these tiny dishes in an infant's grave?

and these silver coins
unearthed from the dirt that used to be a town
images of goddesses and owls and ships and roses
which once passed from hand to hand

and over here a figurine
dark blue bodice and light blue dress
a white shawl draped around her shoulders
the dull red of terracotta showing through faded paint

she's looking quietly down

someone made this and coloured it
someone placed it in a grave because someone else had died
and now a faint echo of a vanished grief
haunts the second shelf up in a labelled glass case

I step outside into sunlight
and follow a signpost down a stony path
to the *Remains of the Temple of Athene*

among pine trees and olives and cypresses

an uneven platform of limestone blocks
elevated a few inches above the dust

AIRPORTS

1

concrete sheds stacked high with pallets
forklifts hauling strings of trailers under arc lights
trucks pull in, pull out
security guards check ID at wire-mesh gates

acres and acres of this

it's not just the millions of tons of concrete
that were mixed and churned and poured
it's not just the cranes, the earth movers
the swarms of men in their hard hats who laboured

but the energy now pulsing through the systems
night and day
the thousands clocking onto and off their shifts
doing the things they've learned how to do

tarmac and Boeings, concrete and radar
a jigsaw all of whose pieces are in people's heads

lights burn night-long in the administration buildings

2

flying from Pokhara to Jomson just after dawn

a light plane built by somebody
which we hope has been serviced by somebody
which is now being flown by someone else
who, we have trusted, knows how to do that

shudders in the updraughts
in the shadowy gorge between Annapurna and Dhaulagiri
then dips towards the airstrip in dawn light
and touches down
bouncing and juddering over rounded boulders in a river bed

the engines are switched off and the door opens
into an enormous silence

high-altitude desert valley
mountains' brown shoulders rising to snowy peaks
huge all around us

thin air
blue sky
faint clank of bells from a distant string of pack horses
coming on a cold breeze across the valley

ELYSIUM BRITANNICUM

John Evelyn

fences and enclosures
knots, parterres and borders
walks, alleys, terraces and bowling greens
groves, labyrinths and pavilions
fountains, canals and spectacular waterworks
rocks and grottoes, mountains and precipices
sundials, urns, statuary and trompe l'oeil painting
music and artificial echoes
hydraulic automata, speaking statues
menageries, apiaries and aviaries
(it is incredible what a concert fifty or sixty birds will produce)

watering
pruning
plashing
nailing
clipping
mowing and rolling

crowns chaplets garlands festoons flower-pots
nosegays
posies
and other flowery pomps

of all terrestrial enjoyments
the most resembling Heaven
and the best representation of our lost felicity

ON THE TRAIN TO SHOREHAM

trees beginning to mist to green
white blossom, pink blossom beside the track
rabbits sit in fields, ears erect in evening sunlight,
not startling as the train goes past

after more than twenty years away
        hearing English in the carriage
and understanding all I hear

the lad in sneakers leafing through the *Sun*
calling on his mobile to see if his horse came in

two grand ladies with cut-glass voices

        well, yes, William does do a good deal of shootin'
        which is why we so often have pheasant on the table

two young women
bare midriffs, snug tops and low-slung jeans

        then, after, I wanted to say, look, I'm really sorry
        I'm really really sorry
        only I switched and I couldn't stop laughing
        well, say it like you mean it, he said
        but I just couldn't help myself

thank you South Central
        no through train today
new rails and sleepers stacked beside the line
a journey taking twice the time it should

        time spent just as well as otherwise

hearing English in the carriage
        trees beginning to mist to green
may blossom, apple blossom beside the track

NEAR PORTHCOTHAN

cottages on a sandy lane
a padlocked out-of-season shop
a path through tamarisks to a headland

salt air, blue sky and running seas
Atlantic winter swell
offshore islands swathed in spray

a beach at the base of granite cliffs
rock stacks, tide-rippled sand
the sea fuming and roiling

a church by an abandoned runway
a village demolished for a 1940s airbase
acres of unkempt grassland

a valley, yellow furze
plank bridge
reed beds and hoofed-up muddy places

the shallow stream empties itself
quietly
over a shingle beach into the ocean

XXI

A SHORT NARRATIVE OF THE RESTAURATION
OF HIS MAJESTY, BY JOHN AUBREY, ESQ., F.R.S.

1

a little before

the Death of Oliver
Protector
a Whale came into the River Thames
and was taken at Greenwich

'tis said Oliver
was troubled at it

2

they could not find any

inclination or propensity
in Generall Monke
to be instrumentall to bring in the King

every night late
I had account of all their Transactions abed

which
like a Sott as I was
I did not while fresh in Memorie
committ to writing

but I remember in the maine
that they were satisfied he had
no more intended or designed the King's
restauration when he came into England
or first came to London

than his Horse did

3

at the (then) Turke's head
in the New Pallace-yard

where was made purposely a large ovall-table
with a passage in the middle
for Miles to deliver his Coffee

about it sat
Mr Harrington's Disciples
and the Virtuosi

the Discourses in this Kind
were the most ingeniose and smart
that I ever heard
or expect to heare
and bandied with great eagernesse

the Arguments in the Parliament howse
were but flatt to it

4

Pride of Senators-for-Life
is insufferable

and they were able
to grind anyone they owed ill will to
to powder

they were hated by
the armie
and the countrey they represented

and their name and memorie stinkes

5

here we had (very formally)
a *Balloting-box*
and balloted how things should be caried
by way of *tentamens*

the room was every evening
full as it could be cramm'd

one time Mr Stafford and his Gang came in
in drink
from the Taverne
and affronted the Junto
(Mr Stafford tore the Orders and Minutes)

the Soldiers offered
to kick them downe stayres

but Mr Harrington's moderation and
persuasion hindred it

6

Mr Harrington was wont
to find fault with the constitution of
our Government

that 'twas *by jumps*

and told a story of a Cavaliero he sawe at the
Carnival in Italie
who rode on an excellent managed horse
that with a touch of his toe would
jumpe quite round

one side of his habit was Spanish
the other French
which sudden alteration of the same person
pleasantly surprized the spectators

just so
said he
'tis with us

7

well
this Meeting continued Novemb. Dec. Jan.
till Febr. 20 or 21

and then upon
the unexpected turne upon Generall Monke's
comeing in

all these aerie modells vanished

8

the multitudes

were so violent
that Generall Monke was almost afrayd of himselfe
and so to satisfie them
(as they use to doe to importunate children)

pray be quiet
yee shall have a free Parliament

this about 7
or rather 8 as I remember
at night

9

immediately a Loud Holla
and shout was given

all the Bells in the Citie ringing and
the whole Citie looked as if it had been in a flame
by the Bonfires
which were prodigiously great and frequent and ran
like a Traine over the Citie
and I saw some Balcones that began to be kindled

they made little Gibbetts
and roasted
Rumpes of mutton

nay I sawe
some very good Rumpes of Beefe

10

well!
a free-Parliament was chosen
and mett

Sir Harbottle Grimston
Knight and Baronet
was chosen Speaker

the first thing he putt to the Question was whether
Charles Steward should be sent for
or no?

yea yea *nemine contradicente*

11

his Majestie and his
Royal Highnesse the Duke of Yorke

all the Gentrie
and Commonaltie of those parts
waiting on them
with great acclamations of Joy &c

12

Mr Harrington's durance
in these Prisons

(he being a Gentleman of a high spirit and a hot head)
was the procatractique cause
of his deliration
or madnesse

which was not outragious

for he would discourse rationally enough
and be very facetious company

but he grew to have a phancy
that his Perspiration
turned to Flies

and sometimes to Bees

13

the Honours conferred on Generall Monke
every one knowes

his sence might be good enough
but he was slow
and heavie

he dyed and
had a magnificent Funerall suitable to
his Greatnesse

14

the return of
his most gracious Majestie

meerly accidental

whatever the
pompous history in 8vo. sayes

SEVEN

(2008–2012)

XXII

THE POETRY OF PLACE

1

thistles among wheat
moor grass in a marshy place beside a canal
across a valley a village vanishes
as a shower draws a veil across the landscape

rain on a blue slate roof
an articulated lorry parked on gravel among puddles

level crossings
small stations on the line across the Vale of York
each with a wooden signal box (manned)
cow parsley and some yellow flowers I don't know the name of

the further west we go the heavier the rain
three wet horses stand motionless in a small green paddock

2

A bosky landskip, passage through which
much delighted all the members of our party.

Mr Gray had brought with him his *Glass*,
a convex, oval mirror with a tinted surface,
with the aid of which he viewed the scene,
afterwards prevailing upon all of us to do the same.

Copses, dells and knolls
lavishly scattered by Nature's gen'rous hand –
yet the very picture of a picture
by that amiable and perfect master, Claude!

Mr Gray instructed us that,
for the glass to work as it ought,
we must turn our backs on the object we wished to view
and screen our eyes from the sun.

3

*One of the country's best preserved castles, a massive fort-
ress with walls nine feet thick.*

*Built between 1378 and 1399 by Lord Richard Scrope,
treasurer and chancellor to King Richard II.*

*Mary Queen of Scots was imprisoned here from 1568 to
1569. Royalists were besieged here during the Civil War.*

*The perfect venue for private functions and corporate
events.*

4

a field of lavender
a rusty disc harrow in the corner of a farmyard
a row of cabin cruisers moored along a river bank
a creosoted fence wet with sudden rain

a fishing boat, mast still erect
sunk to its gunwales in estuary mud
patches of sunlight and a gusty, salty wind
small waves hurrying over rippled sand

the tide ebbs, revealing
embankment masonry course by course
festoons of weed, arches in the stonework
a damp stain marking the spring tide's height

behind the quay
a street of small but handsome Georgian houses
rises to a granite church
and a monument to an 'explorer of the African continent'

a seagull wheels and cries
high over the well-appointed offices
of estate agents and land valuers, investment advisors
solicitors and commissioners for oaths

THE CORNISH HEDGE

I

The Cornish hedge is a hybrid between a stone wall and an earthen bank; it consists of an earth core faced each side with local stone, tapered with an inward curve from the base to halfway up and with bushes or trees growing along its top.

Some hedges date back to the Bronze or Iron Age, others to mediaeval field rationalisations or to the era of the tin and copper boom, when heaths and uplands were enclosed.

Many show by surviving species the habitat that used to surround them: bell heather where moorland was reclaimed, dog's mercury and bluebells where woods were cut.

One to two hundred flowering species and around ten thousand species of insects are usually found in a mile of healthy Cornish hedge, attracting numerous small mammals, birds and reptiles, who come to forage, feed, and build their nests.

2

bird's foot
        bittersweet
                white campion
night-flowering catch-fly

red clover
        hedgerow cranesbill
                ox-eye daisy
field forget-me-not

common fumitory
        purple fumitory
                tall ramping fumitory
western fumitory

goutweed
        autumnal hawkbit
                beaked hawksbeard
cross-leaved heath

early purple orchid
        fool's parsley
                field scabious
common toadflax

English stonecrop
        lesser yellow trefoil
                kidney vetch
weasel's snout

field pansy
        self-heal
                wood sorrel
and common primrose

3

a peculiar whirring, smashing, clattering sound –
a County Highways tractor
with a new machine for trimming hedges

a long box-arm full of whirling flails
sucking into its maw the tide of flowers and busy insects
smashing everything, leaving behind
nothing but a silent bank

scattered along the road
a mess of torn and shredded greenery
thickly strewn with the soft bodies of moths
many cut in half yet still pulsing
a confetti of small bright wings
crushed beetles, dead hoverflies, fragmented bees
disembowelled frogs, little bloody pieces of voles and shrews
crushed silvery bits of slow-worms
pieces of snails, pulped caterpillars
and now and then the tiny paw or tail of a field mouse

of all the grasshoppers that a few moments before
had been flicking out
in front of my dog as he nosed his way along beside the verge
not one could be seen alive

I followed in the wake of the machine
stupidly trying to avoid stepping on the corpses

4

along this mile of Cornish lane
repeated use of the flail has caused the disappearance of

      90 herbaceous species
      5 shrub species
      20 grass species
      60 moss species
      40 bird species
      20 butterfly species
      250 larger moth species
      hundreds of other invertebrate species

since the last yellowhammer flew across the road in 1980
I have never seen another while walking here

since the last grasshopper in July 1981
I have never seen or heard another in these hedges

5

Italian arum (greatly increased, rampant)

hogweed (greatly increased)

ivy (vastly increased, rampant)

Japanese knotweed (greatly increased)

three-cornered leek (greatly increased, rampant)

nettle (greatly increased)

false oat-grass (rampant)

cow parsley (much increased)

rosebay willow-herb (greatly increased, rampant)

bracken (vastly increased, rampant)

AUGUST LINES

> *in memory of Sheila Winifred Rossiter (1925–2008)*
> *and for Mark and Emma*

31 *July* 2008

taking the express from London to York

wheat fields, hedgerows
moor grass in a marshy place beside a canal
across a valley a village vanishes
as a shower draws a veil across the landscape

rain on a blue slate roof
an articulated lorry parked on a gravel road among puddles
(glimpsed as we slow through Doncaster)

alight at York for all stations to Knaresborough and Harrogate
cross a draughty platform under
the high curve of the train shed roof
to a throbbing, rattling two-coach diesel

level crossings and small stations on the branch line
each with a wooden signal box (manned)
cow parsley beside the track
and some yellow flowers I no longer know the name of

1 *August*

walk up Coppice Drive
(visits to school friends in the long summer holidays)
and along the Ripon Road
(discovering *Encounter* in a dentist's waiting room)

past the Cairn Hydro Hotel
(a summer job washing dishes in a basement,
condensation trickling down mould-blackened walls)
and past the Royal Hall

cupolas and pagoda-like towers with green copper roofs
(Emile Ford gyrating to 'Red Sails in the Sunset')
Kursaal elegantly carved in stone above the doorway
(George Melly mugging his way through 'Frankie and Johnny')

walk through the town
seeing what memories present themselves
picking them up, looking at them from different angles
then putting them back in the places they belong

walk up The Ginnel
which really did use to be a ginnel, dark and cobbled
but which now, widened, is just another street
with a café, two bars and an over-priced antique shop

Busby's (now Debenhams) still there on the corner,
Mum and a small myself – after all these years –
still having elevenses in the first-floor tea room
one sunny morning in the 1950s

7 August

on a hilltop beside a pine wood
the three of us take turns to cradle the plastic container
scatter granular ashes among damp bracken
beside a gritstone boulder where
she liked to sit and look out over the valley

drystone walls, brambles,
wind bends the yellowing grasses,
horizon blotted out by low cloud and mist

not by any means an easy life:
a difficult father, a mistaken marriage,
divorce and acrimony
money worries, children brought up single-handed
lonely retirement
arthritis, fragile bones and failing sight

yes, all true – but now
          standing on the hilltop in failing light
I think I sense a different person:
optimistic, ready for anything,
jaunty in her Wren's cap on the quay at Malta
in the early spring of 1945 –

          someone I never really knew
          despite that small framed wartime photo
          on the mahogany dresser in her dining room …

wind combs frail yellow grasses
rain starts to fall

walk down from the hilltop
stop for a moment, look back, and then go on
through fields of thick grass in increasing rain

the beck in spate in the valley bottom
turbulent, dark brown
streaked yellow with mud washed down by the torrent

An hour spent looking through her books: Barry from the charity shop is coming to pick them up tomorrow. In her copy of an Open University textbook, *Culture and Society in Britain* 1850–1890, a quotation from Harriett Taylor Mill's 'Enfranchisement of Women' (1851) is underlined:

We deny the right of any portion of the species to decide for another portion, or any individual for another individual, what is and what is not their 'proper sphere'. The proper sphere for all human beings is the largest and highest which they are able to attain to.

13 *August*, 4 A.M.

Emma in Sheffield, Mark in Sharjah
for me a last night in this flat
awake in the spare room, listening
to a wet gusty wind blowing across miles of Yorkshire

gritstone outcrops high on Blubberhouses Moor
clumps of heather on gnarled black stems

in the wind and rain and darkness
someone's sheep
huddle among cotton grass and tumbled stones
in the lee of a half-ruined drystone wall

13 *August*, 11:30 A.M.

John from Dublin
and the old man he's brought along to help him

boxes and boxes of stuff
heaps of now useless things from the garage
ten minutes to get the wardrobe down the stairs
its plywood then reduced to splinters with an axe
everything goes into the high-sided truck

will the old man survive the day?
a white-haired melancholic ancient
with watering eyes and ashen face

occasionally he stops work
to roll a cigarette and then laboriously smoke it
stands with head bowed while he does so
perfectly still
apart from a faint shaking of the hands

13 *August*, 2 P.M.

the beck looks as it always did
grassy margins, small sandbanks
muddy gaps between trees where the cattle wade
rounded boulders embedded in the stream's smooth flow
the willow tree, on whose limbs
we boys would swing out over the water,
still there, fifty years older, but showing no signs of that

then on up the hill
shadowy pine wood beside me all the way
as I climb to the crest

drystone walls, outcrops of millstone grit
the fields fall steeply to the beck
a silver birch rustles halfway down the slope
the horizon visible today
spiky with the slow gesticulations of a wind farm

I sit on the big flat stone
to feed the living
eating my cheese-and-chutney sandwich

my last time in this place, I suppose

a peaceful place, a beautiful place
to disperse into one's final rest

no sign of any ashes after last week's rain

1 3 *August,* 4 P.M.

the final emptiness of the flat

closing the door on it
turning the key and walking away
waiting on the station's windy platform
starting on a journey to the other end of the country
passing through a green cutting deep in summer grasses
then out across the tall-arched viaduct

Almscliff Crag
that small knuckle of gritstone on its hilltop

    supporting, Andrew Marvell says,
    the heavens on its Atlantean peak

visible from the train as far as Wharfedale
then dropping out of sight

AT HASE-DERA

Sakurai, Nara Prefecture

a Buddha hall high on a mountain side
burnt ten times in a thousand years

a wooden deck built out over a valley
above serried roofs and blossoming trees

a bowl of soba and mountain vegetables
in a cobbled alley near the temple gate

a dead plum tree
another almost as ancient grows beside it

blossoms push out
through the black bark of the trunk itself

XXIII

acres almost cleared of wreckage
here and there a building standing

empty window frames
kitchens without walls, a lampshade swinging in the wind
smashed machinery in a burst-open workshop
dislodged girders, dangling wires

a fishing boat
lies on its side fifty yards from the sea

we're clearing a plot
of the small things left behind by the crane

     video cassette (*The Twilight Samurai*)
     audio cassette (indecipherable)
     fragment of a broken CD (pink, indecipherable)
     nameplate (NAKAMURA)
     rusted kitchen knives
     broken blue crockery
     an elementary student's plastic ruler
     a tube of ketchup

When a plot's been cleared, it's sterilised with a white disinfect-
ant powder; the homeless cats who have outlived their owners
walk across it and then wash their paws, which will make them
sick.

     the tsunami was finally stopped
     by that wooded hill over there beyond the high school
     the first job the next day
     was to disentangle the bodies from the branches

the post office is wrecked
but not the red-painted postbox on its stout single leg –
a car approaches along the potholed road
and stops: a woman rolls down the window
leans out and posts a letter

17–18 *December* 2011

AN UNSEEN CROW

crust of earth
lifted by frost
on stems of fluted ice

cold platform
huddled pigeon
loudspeaker crackling

shopping street muzak
concerto for flute
and pneumatic drill

a stop light quiets
six lanes of traffic
an unseen crow caws

smell of sawn timber
sunny lunch break
carpenters sit and smoke

XXIV

Hemphill, Lake, Bluiett *&* Murray
                (World Saxophone Quartet)
bathing the soul
in the juice of four squeezed saxophones

Monk, spiky and astringent,
constructing a new
and asymmetrical architecture of the ear

Bill Frisell (Mr Pedals) and his Telecaster
conjuring
a phantasmagoria of resonances out of air

genres float through the room
like large benign ghosts

        I have no idea what will happen next

Gil Evans:
'insecurity is the secret of eternal youth'

WEATHERING

storm clouds pulsing in from the Pacific
jolts of lightning, explosive thunder
trees thrash high above the roof in darkness

half a mile away
rain pelts down on Gōtokuji temple and graveyard
(300 *lords, wives, concubines, and children of the Clan of Ii*)

splashing onto
and sluicing off
the Buddha Hall's steep-pitched copper roof

as it has nights like this
for over three hundred years
(wet earth, leaning stones, rain-soaked moss)

who follows
the thread while
letting all manner of things intrude to

     deflect the flow, to
     get included, to be annotated, to
     scatter yet sharpen the attention

wasp on the windowpane
ideas that happen to happen through the door
small outbursts of entertainment vaudeville burlesque
acted out in the theatre of the skull

'all over the place ...'
but always going forward

     a graph of a mind moving...

and even if the grin is a bit fixed

     ('that nice, that clever Mr Whalen!')

the voice nevertheless goes on being
     (in the words of the enthusiastic Mr McClure)
'mock-serious, biting, casual
good-natured, concise, powerful, and humorous'

(did you remember to bring the gin?)

WATCHING BIRDS EAT

mejiro, white-eyes, would come
from their nests
in the tall bamboos to feed

each other berries
in the tree outside our window
each June

but since our neighbour chopped down
his bamboo patch to
enhance the value of his land

not a single one
(bulbuls
steal the berries out of each others' beaks)

REMEMBERING LOL COXHILL

a gathering of England's musical avant-garde
white beards everywhere
good lord, wonderful to see you, are you still alive?

    intermittent drumbeats and cymbal-scrapings

    multiphonic altissimo saxophone drone and flutter

    a power trio disassembles Hendrix

    a guitar played with a bow
    a violin strummed like a guitar
    a singer with a hat made from a cabbage

gathered
in a late-imperial, wood-panelled, high-ceilinged hall
with long purple drapes drawn across the windows

      to commemorate
      a lifetime of commitment to the instant

the passionate, generous
and slightly mad engagement with sound
of one of their own

red plastic bench seats
low lighting and fake marble tables
smooooth-jazz muzak
        (it's painless and you won't hear a thing)
paintings of cattle wading into Highland streams
portions of said cattle at £20 a chunk

        and then, suddenly, on the speakers
        Ella Fitzgerald is singing *Night and Day*

voice
dancing on tiptoe through
        the changes, through the lyrics
inventing any extra notes she needs so she can sing
the song she hears the song suggesting

        1956, thirty-nine years old, at once

a young girl's
        unguarded voice still full of yearning
and the grown woman's full-fledged song
replete with knowledge, balance, poise and joy

mother of all temples and shrines
a *grande dame* who's seen a bit in her time
          Athene, Virgin Mary, mosque, powder magazine
          Venetian artillery, Lord Elgin, UNESCO
floodlit now in all her ruination
a crone with gap-toothed colonnades and fallen pediments

taramosalata, olives, anchovies, butter beans, roast chicken
a robust red wine
photograph (1948) of Seferis and Katsimbalis on the restaurant wall
black pouches under Seferis's eyes

morning, fourth-floor balcony
blue railings, blue awnings, a blue-and-white flag
sun warms my knees
thick yoghurt with honey and nuts, hard-boiled egg
bread and jam and excellent coffee

          you want a traditional Greek breakfast?
          this isn't it?
          oh no! two cups of coffee and five cigarettes

WAITER: *if I had a gun I'd be in prison now*
those politicians in the parliament
they don't even dare go to the window to look out
they and all those other big people stole all the money
and now it's in Latin America somewhere or Switzerland

RECEPTIONIST: *it's no use*
thinking about what happened, we need to think about what's next
so calm yourself

a demonstration assembles
coaches parked in side streets
marchers bussed in from all over the country
     FOR BANK$ BAILING OUT PEOPLE GOT SOLD OUT !!!
scooters and motorbikes with horns sounding
     WALK IN SOLIDARITY
thousands on foot led by drums, banners and loudhailers
applauded from pavements as they pass

shutters, padlocks, FOR RENT signs
the arcades empty
plastic bags blow across marble floors in the shadows

old men sit on straight-backed chairs at the roadside
orange trees line the streets
     dark green foliage full of fruit
men with their hats on gesticulate over thimblefuls of coffee
an old woman bends to tend the lamp in a roadside shrine

Kalamata olives, hummus, beetroot salad, cod with garlic puré
a robust red wine
a photo of the restaurant owner's uncle, killed in Albania, 1940

     written on a wall in Plaka:
     THERE ARE TWO RULES FOR SUCCESS:
     I. NEVER TELL EVERYTHING YOU KNOW

Archaeological Museum
'Mask of Agamemnon'

shock of shining gold verisimilitude

21–24 *November* 2012

PASSING TIME

the sun wheels across the southern sky
and the room that
        – it seems only a moment ago –
was full of light is now in shadow

and we're all that much nearer
        our one irrevocable end
and nothing
of much import has been achieved

Artie the cat
inspects his left forepaw for about a minute
licks it twice
then takes a nap

CROSSING THE THESSALIAN PLAIN

abandoned car dealerships
unfinished houses
the empty shell of a mall
bunches of steel spikes bristle from concrete roofs

crushed cars
and discarded machines
share green fields with imperturbably ruminant goats

1

engraved shields, helmets, breastplates
swords, axes, steel headpieces for horses
crossbows, halberds with six-foot shafts
quivers of steel-tipped arrows
twelve-foot pikestaffs tufted with small red tassels
arquebuses with engraved hexagonal barrels

a chastity belt – late fifteenth century? –
with steel-fanged orifices back and front

(Museo di Palazzo Ducale)

2

Ponte dei Pugni (Bridge of Fists): *From September to Christmas
each year rival clans would gather at bridges without rails and
throw punches with the goal of knocking opponents into the
cold and sewage-strewn canal below. This was tolerated by the
Council of Ten as it marked a big improvement over the earlier
tradition of fights with sharpened and fire-hardened sticks.*

3

Office of the Heads of the Council of Ten:
(no one – not even the accused – may enter the room during a trial)
in the antechamber a *Bocca di Leone*
(Lion's Mouth – for the deposit of denunciations)
next door the State Inquisitors' office
next to that the torture chamber
and so at last to the prisons

VISITING THE ORIENT

step inside to marble pillars, mosaic floor
looping calligraphy on peacock-blue tiles

> *He has created man and taught him speech*
> *He has set the sun and moon in their courses*

a square pond with a trickling fountain
plump diwan cushions
a stuffed peacock
blue-and-white ceramic jars
a stained-glass window with
      a carved and gilded cedarwood frame
inlaid Egyptian woodwork
gilded ceiling, Ottoman chandelier

a *mashrabiyah* (latticework upper-storey window) creating
a *zenana*, a space for modestly peeking women

    Kashan, Damascus, Iznik
    Sind, Kubachi, Cairo, Istanbul

thank you very much, Frederic, Lord Leighton (1830–1896)

as we step out into the twenty-first-century rain
falling steadily on Holland Park Road, London W14

hoar frost on fields and rooftops
        ice-glint in ploughland furrows
trees motionless, angular and bare

in the Quiet Coach riding north
So You Really Want To Learn Latin (Book 1)
        (teenager doing her homework)
'but Mum it *is* turned down'
        (small boy with an iPod Shuffle)

watercolour sky over frozen gravel-pit pools
        heaped detritus of a derelict brickworks
high cirrus skyscape moved by tropospheric winds
        feathery and not to be deflected

ice-bound canal
        frosty floodplain meadow
pearl-grey light tinged with pale gold fire

the midwinter sun drops rapidly westward

Stan Tracey
in dark overcoat, rumpled suit, and Hush Puppies
as of tonight (29th December 2012)
eighty-six-years-minus-one-day old

> ('somewhere deep inside the crusty old cynicism'
> he once said, 'is still
> the bright-eyed lad thinking, *hey this is great!*')

sits down at the piano in the Bull's Head and plays
the particular out-of-tune note *(ouch!)*
he remembers from last month's gig, looks up and remarks

time changes nothing

RECOMMENDING TRISTANO

for Dorsey Kleitz

an email from Dorsey:

> A quick question. Lennie Tristano? I've been reading *The Lonely Voice of Jack Kerouac* where it mentions Tristano was one of Kerouac's favorite jazz pianists. I've never heard of him. Any recommendations, must listens?

flawless technique
perfectly even articulation
underlying steady eighth-note feel
emotionally cool
      (though a much tougher cool than cool-school cool)
structural rigour
a great teacher, the first to teach jazz in a systematic way
influential not only on piano players –
      ladies and gentlemen, please welcome
      Lee Konitz on alto! Warne Marsh on tenor! –
first to record free group improvisations –
      ('Intuition', 'Digression', 1949)
first to use overdubbing, multitracking and
post-production changes of tape speed

      if Charlie Parker is the Schoenberg
      of modern jazz, then Tristano is its Webern
                  (Cook *&* Morton)

following
the path of rhythmic strictness with formidable exactitude

long, angular strings of
almost even eighth-notes provided with
subtle rhythmic deviations and abrasive polytonal effects

a living equilibrium between
forward drive and polyrhythmically-based accenting

    Tristano (Atlantic, 1955)
    The New Tristano (Atlantic, 1961)

on most of the tracks he works with
multiple times
setting 5/4 or 3/8 or some other time against a steady 4/4
and producing astonishing contours made up of, say

    4 on 3 (in one hand)
        on top of 5 on 4 (in the other hand)
          on top of 4/4 (the basic beat)

what I care about is that the result sounded good to me

I can never think and play at the same time — it's an emotional impossibility

XXV

1

an early morning walk, passing
three-bedroom houses, balconied mansion blocks,
    a market gardener's plot sown with cabbages –
following the line of cherry trees that follows
the course of the concrete-covered river

    where *hiyodori, suzume, mejiro* –
    brown-eared bulbuls, sparrows, white-eyes –
    shriek, chirp, or flit in and out of bushes

to Setagaya Hachiman shrine
founded by Minamoto no Yoshiie (Shogun) in 1091

'the god of eight banners' – of warriors, war, and archery

square vermilion pillars, horned gables
a curved roof of overlapping copper tiles
renovated in 1546
by Kira Yoriyasu, lord of Setagaya

    swept gravel precinct
    kuromatsu, kashi, kaya, keyaki
    black pines, evergreen oaks, nutmegs, zelkovas

river boulders –
力石: *chikara-ishi*, 'strength-stones', says the sign –
    nested like eggs on a bed of white gravel, each
    engraved with the stone's deadweight
    and the name of the man who had lifted it

an intense-looking high-school boy climbs
the granite steps to the shrine
bows and claps – and prays and prays and prays

2

back on the street: bakery and beauty parlour
        (a satchelled schoolgirl runs by, late for class)
convenience store, second-hand clothes shop
        (a housewife waters her wall-top potted plants)
bright tram tracks laid on weedy ballast
        (a bent old woman sweeps her doorstep)
an antique streetcar
preserved by the tramstop for kids to play in

an avenue of leaning pines leads to
the gate of Gōtokuji
                    (Zen temple, Sōtō sect)

        founded by Kira Masatada
        in memory of his aunt, who died in 1480

three gilded statues sit
in the silence and shadow of the Buddha Hall

3

the Kiras defeated by Toyotomi Hideyoshi in 1590
and their castle (just down the road) destroyed

        leafy mound, dry moat
        park benches and a public toilet
        cicadas shrilling in summer heat

Setagaya later given by Tokugawa Ieyasu to Ii Naomasa
for services rendered by his troops
        (blood-red armour, the 'Red Devils of Ii')
at the battle of Sekigahara (1600)

Gōtokuji thereafter the family temple of the Ii:
        eaves, roof-beams, water-tubs –
their crest is everywhere

4

buried here is Ii Naosuke
who with Commodore Townsend Harris
on the deck of the USS Powhatan signed
        the 'Treaty of Amity and Commerce' (1858)
and who for his pains was cut to pieces by seventeen samurai
at the Sakurada Gate of the Imperial Palace
24 March 1860

        a stone column on a carved lotus-flower base
        in a stone enclosure – stone
        fence posts, stone doors, the entrance flanked
        by stone lanterns capped with moss

a metal plaque gives the details of his story
his grave still frequently visited

Setagaya: forty-two villages
rice paddies
wheat, millet, cotton, hemp, sweet potato fields
oranges, mulberry, tea, bamboo

labour in the fields in summer
make straw boots and cloaks in winter
plait straw ropes, mend clothes, pound rice

cotton kimono, loin cloth, straw sandals

the annual tax collector's visit
        (land tax 40–50% of the harvest)
taxes on doors, windows, cloth,
saké, hazel trees, beans and hemp

sesame seeds and peasants are very much alike
the more you squeeze them the more you can extract from them

infestation, pests, blight, drought, typhoon

if a farmer leaves his field, either to engage in trade, or to work
for hire, not only must he be punished, but the whole village
must be indicted with him – Hideyoshi (1591)

husbands hold the family seal
wives the rice scooper

no family names allowed by law
none of their given names now known

VISITING THE ANCESTORS

1

brisk sea wind, a red-brick path beside
        a semicircle of sandy beach
long shadows in evening sunlight
        freighters heading in and out of Kobe
a green-painted Taisho-Era villa with octagonal tower,
sage-green shutters and steep Dutch-gabled roof,
its eccentric elegance dwarfed by
        the 300-metre-high concrete towers
of the world's longest single-span suspension bridge
soaring high above the choppy strait to Awaji-shima

we take Maya's gentle eighty-three-year-old father
        (ex-merchant seaman, Esperanto speaker, communist)
for a spin along the seafront in his wheelchair
        (cancer, two strokes, heart attack, but he still keeps going)
he points left and says *turn right*
he points right and says *turn left*
he points straight ahead and says
        my head isn't working properly any more

2

okonomiyaki restaurant where we're the only customers
and where the owner
        sixty-two years old and still a beauty
has been hitting the *shochu* cocktails –
almost too drunk to cook, but she manages in the end
after frequent reminders about what we'd ordered

she talks a lot, switching between
Japanese and lightly inflected NHK-acquired English –
    I wanted to learn it because
      when I was at junior high I used to wonder if I was a haafu –
and occasionally breaks into short sequences
of sexy dance-steps
      spatulas held high like handkerchiefs or castanets
as she shimmies behind the sizzling hotplate

she won't let us pay for our drinks because
she's had such a good time, and because
she well remembers Maya's favourite aunt
who, thirty years ago, kept the sweetshop down the road

3

waterside hotel, grey morning,
bullrushes, sedge,
raindrops winking rings on the water's surface,
electric-blue flash of a kingfisher low across the pond

4

Suma, where
after the defeat of the Heike in 1184
the flute player Taira no Atsumori
sixteen or seventeen years old
    with a lightly powdered face and blackened teeth
was killed on the beach
    (a boy just the age of his own son)
by Kumagai Naozane

a haiku by Basho inscribed on a stone
in the temple garden:

> *oh, Suma-dera*
> *listening to the no-sound of the flute*
> *in the darkness under the trees*

and another by Buson:

> *the waves*
> *attracted by the sound of the flute —*
> *Suma in autumn*

the flute itself is in the temple's treasure house

5

remove withered stalks from the vases
replace them with green *sakaki*, refresh the water
light incense sticks, pour water on the stone
never ask the ancestors for anything, just thank them

grandfather, third son of a landowner
fell in love with a geisha
married her and was disinherited
fathered twelve children then died of a stroke at forty
Ryoichi, the eldest son, took on the father's role
called up in 1942
he sent his mother letters from wherever he was posted

> a 500 lb. bomb
> through the steel-plate deck
> of a troop transport en route for Manila

for the rest of her life
periodically
she locked herself away and reread all his letters

        which were cremated with her, their ash
        mingled with hers under the stone

pour more water
over the smooth wet shining granite

6

train back to Tokyo
look up to see
rows of prefabricated houses straddling a hillside
their windows looking down
        on flooded paddy fields and
the white flash of our Shinkansen racing between two tunnels

LOOKING AT THE CITY
                FROM PARLIAMENT HILL

1

a kestrel wheels and hovers
        above grass and woodland
a siren's wail floats up from Kentish Town
a retriever noses scents through tangled bushes

against a hazy pearl-grey sky
        stained citron on the eastern horizon
the skyline of Canary Wharf and the City
is a double-peaked bar graph, illustrating
        a nasty recession between two chunky booms

        look, son
        that's where the money lives and breeds

assets, ambition, anxiety, algorithms
fermenting in their steel and glass housings

2

when the call comes people know right away: we may use the
most innocent tone of voice when we say: 'hi, could you pop up
to the 20th floor for a moment?' – they know better, you never
get an unexpected call from that person unless …

after our conversation, which typically lasts five minutes, they
will be led out of the building by security

3

three days later, a sunny Sunday,
         the hill is crowded –
joggers, strollers, lovers, toddlers,
         bibliophiles on benches,
dogs in hot pursuit of sticks and tennis balls

the sky is criss-crossed with
         a loosely woven web of contrails
dispersing softly
high above the distant shells of concrete, steel and glass

which are quiet today
hundreds of thousands of blank screens and unoccupied desks

a security guard patrols an empty corridor

bars of light and shade
         shift through silent offices
as the sun dips
south-westwards over deepest Hampshire

up from the tube into Threadneedle Street
carved pediments
          and Corinthian columns
dark suits displaying poppies
          shoulder to shoulder with those who Serve
a lunchbar chalkboard
sandwiches, coffee, Moët *&* Chandon (£59)

          lone figures in alleys and under arches
          feed
          on smartphone screens and cigarettes

on past The Monument (to the Great Fire of 1666)
the better to preserve the memory of this dreadful visitation
28,196 cubic feet of Portland stone at a cost of £13,450 11s 9d
with a viewing platform at a height of 202 feet, from which

          John Cradock (a baker)
          Lyon Levi (a diamond merchant)
          Leander (a baker)
          Margaret Moyes (the daughter of a baker)
          Robert Donaldson Hawes (a fifteen-year-old boy)
          and Jane Cooper (a servant-girl)

leapt, between 1788 and 1842, to their deaths
the gallery thereafter enclosed in an iron cage

and so pass on
          to Lower Thames Street
no public bar chatter, no whining of a mandolin
audible above the insistence of the traffic

          inexplicable splendour of Ionian white and gold
          closed today
          we are sorry for any inconvenience

two middle-aged women
        deep in conversation
            demo ne ... so ne ...
a teenage girl (daughter of one, niece of the other?)
sits opposite them
fiercely scanning a fashion magazine

liqueur bottles
        stand to attention on the fridge top
chocolate cake
slightly slumped in the dessert cabinet

three model dogs –
one six inches high and two at half that height – sit
        in attitudes of unqualified devotion
on the plastic shelving beside the till

chatty waitress
the differences between Pacific and Atlantic fish
good that my Japanese seems to be holding up so well
even though I can't just now for the life of me recall
        what kind of fish めかじき (*mekajiki*) might be
(swordfish I remember later)

ano ne ... so ne ... demo ne ...
        the magazine consumed
the teenager
sits in chin-on-hand glazed-eye rebellious silence

a plate of
sausage-and-spring-cabbage cream-sauce spaghetti
arrives on my red-check tablecloth
        (could that be a smell of mint?)
accompanied by a large glass of unexpectedly excellent wine

XXVI

Richard Carew of Antony, *The Survey of Cornwall*, 1602

Saltash

seated
    on the declyning of a steep hill
the towne consisteth of three streets
       which every showre washeth cleane
compriseth between 80. and 100. households
underlyeth the government of a Maior *&* his 10. brethren
and possesseth sundry large priviledges over the whole haven

to wit
an yeerely rent of boates and barges appertayning to the harbour
ancorage of strange shipping
crowning of dead persons, laying of arrests
and other Admirall rights

here dwelleth one *Grisling*
deafe from a long time, who hath
a strange quality to understand what you say
(contrary to the rules of nature and yet without the helpe of arte)
by marking the moving of your lips

I had almost forgotten to tell you that
there is a well in this towne
whose water
will never boyle peas to a seasonable softnes

Launceston

those buildings commonly knowne by the name of Launston
and written Lanceston
are by the *Cornishmen* called *Lesteevan*
(*Lez* in *Cornish* signifieth broad, *&* those are scatteringly erected)

they are governed by
a Maior and his scarlet-robde brethren

there is
adjoynant in site but sequestred in jurisdiction
an ancient Castle whose steepe rocky-footed Keepe
hath his top environed with a treble wall

and in regard thereof
men say was called

Castle Terrible

Bodmin

in *Cornish, Bos venna*
commonly termed Bodman
which (by illusion if not Etimology)
a man might not unaptly turne into Badham
for of all the townes in Cornwall I hold
none more contagiously seated than this

it consisteth wholly of one street
whose South side is hidden from the Sunne by an high hill
so neerly coasting it in most places as neither can
light have entrance to their staires
nor open ayre to their other roomes

their back houses
of more necessary than cleanly service
as kitchins, stables, &c.
are clymed up unto by steps, and their filth
by every great showre
washed downe through their houses into the streetes

Tintagel

more famous for his antiquite
than regardable for his present estate

(yet the ruines
argue it to have been once
no unworthie dwelling for the *Cornish* princes)

halfe the buildings
were raised on the continent and
the other halfe on an Iland

in passing thither
you must first descend with a dangerous declyning
and then make a worse ascent by a path
      through his sticklenesse occasioning and
      through his steepnesse threatning
the ruine of your life with the failing of your foote

at the top
two or three terrifying steps give you
entrance to the hill
which supplieth pasture for sheepe and conyes

Padstow

a towne and haven of sutable quality
for both (though bad)
are the best that the north *Cornish* coast possesseth

the harbor is barred with banks of sand
        made (through uniting their weake forces)
sufficiently strong to resist
        the Ocean's threatning billows
which (divorced from their parent)
find their rage subdued
by the other's lowly submission

Mr *Nicholas Prideaux* from his new
and stately house thereby
taketh a ful and large prospect of
the towne, haven *&* countrey adjoyning

to all which his wisdome is a stay
his authority a direction

Wadebridge

the salt water leaving Padstowe
floweth up into the countrey that it may
embrace the river Camel, and
having performed this naturall courtesie
ebbeth away againe to yield him the freer passage

by which meanes
they both undergoe Wade bridge
the longest, strongest and fayrest that the Shire can muster

Lostwithiel

Maioralty, markets, faires
and nomination of Burgesses for the parliament
it hath in common with the most

Coynage of Tynne
onely with three others
but the gayle for the whole
Stannary and keeping of the County Courts
it selfe alone

yet all this can hardly
rayse it to a tolerable condition of wealth and inhabitance

wherefore I will detayne you no longer

THE CORNISH HOUSE

Richard Carew of Antony, *The Survey of Cornwall*, 1602

1

the ancient maner of *Cornish* building was
     whereas now-adayes they
to plant their houses lowe
     seat their dwellings high
to lay the stones with morter of lyme and sand
     lay them with earthen morter
to make the walles thick
     build their walles thinne
to make their windowes arched and little
     mould their lights large
to frame the roomes not to exceede two stories
     raise them to three or foure stoaries
seeking therethrough onely strength and warmnesse
     coveting chiefly prospect and pleasure

2

for covering of Houses, there are three sorts of Slate
the first and best, Blew:
in substance thinne, in colour faire
in waight light, in lasting strong

the Sea strond also in many places affordeth
Peebble-stones, which
are by often rolling of the waves wrought to a kind of roundnesse
and serve verie handsomely for paving of streetes and Courts

3

the poore Cotagers content themselves with
Cob for their wals and Thatch for their covering
few partitions, no planchings or glasse windows
and scarcely any chimnies
other then a hole in the wall to let out the smoke

straw and blanket
a mazer and a panne or two comprise all their substance

THE INVENTION *of the* LAKE DISTRICT

Thomas Gray to Dr Thomas Wharton, 1769

I

walk'd over a spungy meadow or two
& began to mount the hill thro' a broad
& straight green alley among the trees
& with some toil gained the summit
& from hence saw the Lake majestic in its calmness, clear
& smooth as a blew mirror with winding shores
& low points of land cover'd with green inclosures
& white farm houses looking out among the trees
& cattle feeding

descended again by a side avenue
& continued my way along the shore, close to the water
& generally on a level with it
& saw a cormorant flying over it
& fishing

2

our path tends here to the left
& the ground gently rising
& cover'd with a glade of scattering trees
& bushes on the very margin of the water

then opens both ways the most
delicious view that my eyes ever beheld

behind you are the magnificent heights of *Walla*-crag
& opposite lie the thick hanging woods of Ld Egremont
& *Newland*-valley with green
& smiling fields embosom'd in the dark cliffs

& to the left the jaws of *Borodale*
& that chaos of mountain behind mountain roll'd in confusion
& beneath you the shining purity of the *Lake*, ruffled by the breeze
& reflecting rocks, woods, fields
& inverted tops of mountains
& with the white buildings of *Keswick*, *Crosthwaite*-church
& *Skiddaw* for a back-ground at distance

oh Doctor!

I never wish'd more for you – & pray think
how the glass played its part in such a spot!

3

soon after we came under *Gowder*-crag
a hill more formidable to the eye
& to the apprehension than that of *Lodoor*

the rocks atop
deep-cloven perpendicularly by the rains, hanging loose
& nodding forwards, seem just starting from their base in shivers

the whole way down
the road on both sides is strew'd with piles of the fragments
strangely thrown across each other
& of dreadful bulk

the place reminds one of those passes in the Alps
where the Guides tell you to move on with speed
& say nothing
lest the agitation of the air should loosen the snows above
& bring down a mass, that would overwhelm a caravan

I took their counsel and hasten'd on in silence
non ragioniam di lor; ma guarda, e passa

4

in the evening walk'd alone down to the lake
by the side of *Crow-Park* after sunset

& saw the solemn covering of night draw on
the last gleam of sunshine fading away on the hill-tops
the deep serene of the waters
& the long shadows of the mountains thrown across them
till they nearly touch'd the hithermost shore

at distance heard the murmur
of many waterfalls not audible in the day-time

wish'd for the Moon, but she was
dark to me & silent, hid in her vacant interlunar cave

5

the road in some parts made, in others
dangerous for carriages, slippery
& stony, but no precipices

a very beautiful view down the Lake

the inhabitants pronounce the name
of *Skiddaw-fell* with a sort of terror and aversion

a little to the west a stone bridge of 3 arches
here I dined at an inn that stands there

the sky was overcast
& the wind cool

several little showers today

said to be snow on *Cross-fell*

6 ·

from the shore a low promontory pushes itself far into the water
& on it stands the white village of *Grasmere*
with the parish-church rising in the middle of it

hanging inclosures
corn-fields
& meadows as green as an emerald with their trees
& hedges
& cattle
fill up the whole space from the edge of the water
& just opposite to you is a large farmhouse
at the bottom of a steep smooth lawn embosom'd in old woods
wch climb half-way up the mountain's side
& discover above them a broken line of crags, that crown the scene

not a single red tile
no flaring Gentleman's house
or garden walls
break in upon the repose of this little unsuspected paradise
all is peace, beauty
& happy poverty in its neatest most becoming attire

WORDS BY SAMUEL PALMER & HIS SON HERBERT

Samuel Palmer's eldest son, Thomas More Palmer, died in 1861 at
the age of 19; after Palmer's own death in 1881, his younger son,
Alfred Herbert Palmer, wrote and edited *The Life and Letters of
Samuel Palmer, Painter and Etcher,* which was published in 1892.

1

outlines cannot be got too black

we must not begin with medium
but think always on excess
and only use medium to make excess more abundantly excessive

we are not troubled with aerial perspective in the valley of vision

2

a certain sentiment of surpassing fruitfulness

*if nature has been consulted
it has been consulted as it were in a distorting glass*

*a huge bank of cumulus clouds which look
        (as Mr Hook says of the cumuli of Cadore)
as if you could knock your head against them*

*bright crimson apples so numerous and so enormous
        as far to surpass the utmost stretch of possibility
a tremendous and utterly abnormal crop*

(bits of nature
are generally much improved by being received into the soul)

*he could not have passed the most absurdly elementary examination
in botany, entomology, ornithology, or geology*

(exhibitions
of clover and beans and parsley and mushrooms and cow dung
and the innumerable etceteras of a foreground)

3

a nice tight armful of a spirited young lady

Italy
especially Rome
is quite a new world

I can never paint in my old style again

4

today the first snow has fallen on our dear boy's grave

what is called a beautiful view gives me
no more real pleasure than the contemplation

of a kitchen sink

5

forswear HOLLOW compositions like Calypso and St Paul
and forswear great spaces of sky

TAKE SHELTER IN TREES

*(an almost feminine want of reticence
in matters relating to his feelings, griefs and disappointments)*

Thursday, rose without much horror

a living inhumement
and equal to the dread throes of suffocation, turning
this valley of vision into a fen of scorpions and stripes and agonies

MISERABLY HAMPERED

though nobody will believe it
because I am round in the waist
and the corners of my mouth turn up naturally

Yours affectionately, The Most Unhappy of Men, S. Palmer

PIET MONDRIAN IN BELSIZE PARK

> Letters (1938–1940) from 60 Parkhill Road NW3 to
> Winifred Nicholson in Cumberland and, after 1939,
> to Ben Nicholson and Barbara Hepworth in St Ives.

1

I am always glad to be here!
the air is good for my health but above all
the spiritual surroundings here is better than in Paris to me

2

I have difficulty with an ear and the nose
Dr Coburg took wax out of one of them but
a noise remains in the other

and then the nose began to be wrong
one nose hole is too narrow and already 20 years ago
I suffered with it

3

haven't you suffered of the cold?
I only a few days by that great wind

after the snow falling the heating is sufficient
against such a wind is nothing

4

my work goes better than ever

5

Mr Morton
made the impression on me as if there was no war at all

that was a little strange to me
I think one must suffer when all are suffering

perhaps Mr Morton is too young to me

6

I am so late to answer you because
I had so much to do

only making the black-out with little costs
took me 2 weeks

7

even I began a new composition (small)

and also an article in relation with the world situation:
'Art Shows the Evil of Totalitarian Tendencies'

perhaps it may be of use

8

since Paris fell
I did no more creative work

the day is too near

might the Nazis come in, what then?
my article won't do me much good, neither

9

I am trying to get a visa to New York

I should have liked to see you before
but I don't think I succeed with getting out
it will be too late

10

I have not lost confidence in Human's future
and Progress

and for we make part of that Progress
perhaps we will overcome the darkness

11

I suffered from intestines-troubles caused by the liver
every week I was at the doctor
nearly better
I got a little fishbone in the throat that bothered me much

then my windows were blown in
(fortunately I had my black-out
but shutters were blown half open all the same!)
by a bomb a little farther in Parkhill rd

I was on bed but had only dust in an eye

lucky!

12

yesterday I took my valises
out up here in Ormonde-Hôtel where I stay
untill I go

here there is a good shelter under the hôtel

I do like your photo of relief
only I should like the big round a little otherwise placed
it goes to the left

your old friend Mondrian

I believe in our end victory!

XXVII

MARY CELESTE

a text abandoned by

almost in the middle of

the language not entirely

the sentences strangely

the words show no signs of

we find ourselves unable to

the silence is undeniably

the page has been laid out as if

HOMAGE TO WCW

weeds and leafless vines
scattered

brownish
no signs of life

what's to be done with all
this dried-up verbiage?

the doctor
drives past the field

on his way to
the contagious hospital

the words, rooted,
grip down, begin to awaken

ARS POETICA

languaged,
moving through

(affected by
and affecting)

a locale (itself
always in transition),

noticing what's there
to be noticed,

shaping the traces into
an asymmetrical

verbal object that can
stand on its own

feet – however many of
those there turn out

to be – the shaping
of the language being

the shaping of the world
that shapes the self

that shapes the world that
shapes the poem

BONFIRE OF THE ADJECTIVES

arched arched	huge huge
bald	knobbly
belabouring	long long
blue	overwhelmed
bristling	reliable
cool	salty
clustered	scruffy
deep deep deep	silent
deft	small small small
detached	squeaky
discarded	steel-clad
domed	swift
driven	tempered
feathered	toothed
frozen	tree-lined
gleaming	tusked
glowing	unimpeded

safely removed from twenty-six older poems, January 2013

He fucks you up, that Larkin bloke,
    he means to, and he does it well,
palming off his self-dislike
    as every living person's hell.

He was fucked up too, of course,
    before he sat down at his desk
to give diminishment a voice
    and rewrite life as Larkinesque.

He spreads his misery far and wide,
    it's bad for everybody's health,
stop reading him is my advice
    and never write such stuff yourself.

EIGHT

(2012–2019)

XXVIII

PYTHAGOREAN

straighten the bed clothes on rising
and smooth out the place where you lay

spit on your hair clippings and nail parings
destroy the mark of the pot in the ashes

don't look in a mirror by lamplight
nor stir the fire with a knife

don't turn around at the border
for surely the Furies are following

struck bronze sings with the voice
of the daemon captive within it

the Pleiades are the lyre of the Muses
and the planets are Persephone's dogs

In a field that slopes to the cliff edge
a farmer stops his tractor at the end of a furrow,
turns off the engine, sits, and watches the sea
as a south-westerly wind buffets his cab.

A cultural geographer, the wind in his face,
Deleuze and Merleau-Ponty in his pack,
walks along the coast path, thinking:
There's nothing really to say about the sea
except what we already know from looking at it –
it's always different, always the same.

The farmer paints on Sundays.
He tries to paint the sea, to capture the way
waves behave as they break – but how to do it?
No two waves he's seen were ever the same.

The geographer reaches the headland,
takes notebook and pen from his pocket
and writes on a wind-ruffled page:
Or, rather, it is composed of innumerable differences
so finely different that their
incessant production is also their apparent erasure.

EN ROUTE

AT NARITA

airport hotel room:
a blank through which purposes
pass without friction

SERVICE NON COMPRIS

led to table by
high heels and long legs, served by
starched cuffs and haircut

IMPERIAL

Roman statue: de-
tachable head (emperor
changes, change the head)

ART AND ECONOMICS

lads with loads of time
derelict factory fence
such fine graffiti

IN PROVENCE

silence, dust and sun,
a hot car parked on gravel
by a crumbling wall

SEA-CHANGE

brine-pits
and broom-groves

cloud-capped
dew-lapped
and dove-drawn

ever-angry
ever-harmless

heart-sorrow
honey-drops
and horse-piss

inch-meal
lass-lorn
never-surfeited

sea-marge
sea-sorrow
sea-swallowed

sight-outrunning
spell-stopped
and still-vexed

thunder-claps
thunder-stroke

up-staring
urchin-shows

wave-worn
and weather-fended

ISLANDED

dark blue, whitecapped
waves fill the lower half of the window

heathery hills the upper half, and then

as the boat rolls, the window
frames only sky

*

approaching the island

a hundred yards offshore
the smell of cow shit on the wind

*

a curve of beach
a jetty
a low rounded hill
leaning gravestones and a roofless chapel

     await the thick deft BB pencil
     of Wilhelmina Barns-Graham

*

horizontal bands of colour
reach to a low horizon:

a drystone wall spotted with yellow lichen
a brilliant strip of grass
a fire-red straggle of wind-blown montbretia
slick black rain-wet tarmac
        richly smirched by the recent passage
        of a trotting herd of beeves
ribbons of yellow and brown seaweed
ruffled water tinged turquoise by the sandy seabed
        darkening further out to deeper then deeper blues

on the opposite shore
banks of mottled brown seaweed slope up to
red-roofed houses and a gently curved horizon
where two wind turbines stand tall against grey sky

        small boats heave at their anchors
                in an insistent westerly wind
        seabirds bob among whitecaps

        cloud shadows and sunshine
        constant changes of light

low grey clouds head rapidly eastwards
high white altocumuli proceed steadily west

*

connoisseurs by now
of squall, downpour and drench

        (*you'll be all right atween the shoures*
        the Papa Westray boatman said as we disembarked)

weather sweeps in from the west
wind so strong it blows the pelting rain
horizontally over our heads as we hunker
        in the lee of the half-height walls
of the oldest house in north-west Europe

dry and snugly sheltered, squatting on our heels
on a Neolithic farmer's living room floor

*

people friendly, grounded
        always ready for a chat
somewhere where everyone knows everyone

        swadge: to sit back and rest after eating

        'four' pronounced *phooerr*

Michael's family:
here on the island since the eleventh century

*

*The bakery bakes bread on Wednesday and Saturday — you get
it hot from the oven. They can't easily send it off the island. It's
a matter of sustainability — you don't want to build up your
workforce, and then the winter storms are bad enough so there's
no boats, and then you lose all the contracts. So they mostly make
biscuits and oat-cakes and things with a longer shelf-life — a
week of storms with no boats makes no difference to those.*

*

curlews, lapwings, snipe, golden plovers and linnets
feed in the fields

grey seals
                with white whiskers
sit up head and shoulders out of the water
watch us with alert and curious eyes

fulmars, gannets and gulls soar above the sea
rise on updrafts, wheel on gusts, or
let their flight be
                        slowly bent from its path
by the unabating, incessant westerly

> *beak, bird-eye and ruffled feather*
> *the weather-wise tilt of a slanted wing*
> *my song my flight a wind-blown silence*
> *poised on a swerve of air*

*

in the small
airport
departure lounge

the clock
is wrong

Westray & Papa Westray, 12–14 September 2018

XXIX

NORTH

the train halts

windless silence, falling snow
visibility ten metres

twigs and branches, silver
birches muffled with heavy white

*

north-western coast
a sea in turmoil
among dark rocks

*

FUROUFUSHI ONSEN

a concrete path across a stony beach
        yukata flapping wildly in the gale
to an open-air hot spring exactly at
the sea's edge

        waves heave towards the land,
        sheets of foam criss-cross,
        overtake each other, subside
        in an agitation of blue water
        amongst black rocks beside the bath

steaming orange-brown
                mineral-laden water
a pink-orange sunset intermittently glimpsed
between grey roiling clouds

gulls swerve and dip
three rapid cormorants
    do a fly-by parallel to the shore

biting wind off the sea chills
the windward shoulder
fingers and toes
instantly numb on stepping from water into air

    furoufushi = 'no ageing, no death'

*

the gale thumps, batters at
the flimsy building all night
loud enough to wake me, take me
to the window to watch

huge seas crashing to shore
waves tripping over
themselves and tumbling headlong
in a seethe of white

in the grey dawn
a hailstorm rattles the breakfast room windows

*

MORNING BUS

coastal villages
potholes and empty houses
no one to be seen

*

wind strong enough to have rolled newly fallen snow
into snowballs, to have trundled these across the
freezing white plain – leaving a tangled
skein of tracks behind them – until,
too heavy to be shifted further,
they came to rest, stranded
here and there in their
random not-random
places

*

AOMORI

apples and grown-under-snow carrots
fish from northern ports

in the hush after
the shinkansen's departure
boot soles creak on snow

Akita & Aomori Prefectures, 28–29 January 2019

LOCAL INGREDIENTS

WELCOME TO PANSY SATELLITE

      – sign over a shoe shop in the
underground passage at Shinjuku station

red cardboard speech bubbles
affixed to pert red ankle boots say:

      HOT !!!

– and so to L'AMBRE coffee shop
a plush and lofty-ceilinged basement
whose tobacco-stained stucco walls,
            rustic red-brick pillars, fake marble tables
                        and low red-velvet-cushioned chairs
are lit by triple-decker wrought-iron chandeliers
suspended from dusty metal chains

            Beethoven plays from the speakers –
            and here we are,
                              effortlessly transported
            fifty years back to the late Showa Era

*

Karasuyama-gawa
                        a former semi-rural
watercourse, confined under concrete, now
a paved and shrub-lined
            footpath snaking through the suburbs

an old man plods along it
a dinging bear-bell dangling from
his daypack, memento
of long-gone days of Alpine derring-do

afternoon: to the dentist
root canal work
two front teeth at the bottom are under threat:
will I be able to keep them?

(doubtful)

once upon a time I was a 'young man'
now I'm an 'older person'

*

at Someday in Shinjuku:
        Takeuchi Nao's nine-piece band
four seasoned players (tenor, trombone, baritone, drums)
the other five in their twenties, all
                with idol-style mop haircuts
(the two trumpeters growing thin moustaches)
faultless reading (complex charts) and brimming-over solos

the generosity of jazz!
its endlessly inventive gifting

(what I spotted as a teenager, listening to
Tubby Hayes and Ronnie Scott
        in the basement at 39 Gerrard Street –
and it's kept me hooked all these years)

I order a bottle of wine: Mo has to go out
and get one from the convenience store –
        the economics of owning a live house:
his middle names Precarity and Jazz

*

whenever I walk
through the underground passage between
the two subway stations at Shinjuku San-chome
        as I do on my way home tonight
        (the route we took together evening and morning)
I remember Alison, it happens every time

        the young Ali, 1981

(especially tonight I remember her now anew:
last year, so suddenly, leukaemia)

*

to the hospital in Ogikubo to see Dr Nishino,
set an appointment for the annual post-cancer check, get
the ECG, blood test, and X-ray done,
the hospital staff as always
                unfailingly cheerful and friendly
a saintly profession

        walking back to the station
        Tokyo winter sunlight on my face
        glinting, brilliant, clear

*

Fuji-san looms when seen from
        the platform at Kyodo station
this evening especially, silhouetted against
an orange sky
a horizontal band of cloud
edged with sunset fire encroaching on one flank

*

a flawless violet evening sky
bathes the Meiji-era
red brick façade of Tokyo Station in light

across the street
shining glass towers float high above
        five-storey early-Showa buildings of cut stone
        inside whose emptied shells
        the bases of the skyscrapers have been inserted

pass through glass doors into one of these
        then up the escalator to the Cotton Club
where everything narrows down to a small pool of light
containing Marcin Wasilewski
            playing 'Night Train to You' –

    touch, definite and delicate
    strong and, at once, gentle –

            the way, when he
            completes an intricately
            serpentine
            phrase in the
            treble, he suddenly
            raises his right elbow high

*

a beautiful February spring-like day
train to Yokohama
where I get lost in the enormous station (as I always do)
lunch with Bill Elliott
he's writing a lot, his swansong he calls it (he's 87)

train to Kamakura, narrow-gauge to Hase

       such handsome houses in Kamakura
       even the ones with plastic façades
       look as if they might have been designed
       rather than put together from a kit

crowds of tourists at the great Buddha
       (the road from the station
more commercial than it used to be, I notice)

         up a steep path at the back of the temple
         a peaceful sunlit
         walk through trees once I get my breath back

narrow-gauge home along the shore

       late-afternoon sunlight on the
       inward-rolling, long-fetch, deep-blue, silky Pacific swell

*

Kobe
to meet Maya's mother at
the hospital where her father goes for day care

     a short walk after lunch while
         mother and daughter talk some more
     downhill to a cemetery, where
     I perch on a boulder in the sunshine –

odd to be sitting quietly in a graveyard with none of whose in-
habitants I have any connection, here on the other side of the
world – although that of course begs the question:

            which side of the world is 'other'?

     a satisfaction, a kind of peace
     in actually being here in a place
     I never imagined I would visit
     that I didn't know existed
     and which I'll never come back to

at the hospital
we wheelchair Maya's father to the café for tea

     most of what he says
     incomprehensible because of the stroke
     but he wolfs down a waffle with evident pleasure

father and daughter are delighted to see each other
Maya has brought him a bag of books

*

in Takamatsu
dinner in a restaurant
where Isamu Noguchi used to be a regular

      richly coloured, grainy wooden tables
      modernist curves, planes and angles

Noguchi lampshades (originals) – small
suspended sculptures of thick
      white handmade paper

a restaurant catering for
fans of Modernism (like us) or
      (white shirt, sedge hat, walking staff)
pilgrims visiting the eighty-eight temples of Shikoku

the cook uses only local ingredients

   *

in the morning, the route from
the station to the Noguchi Museum
passes across the site of the Battle of Yashima (1185)
      a naval encounter although
        now it's all reclaimed land

a roadside plaque tells us that
right here, on this piece of potholed tarmac,
      Nasu no Yoichi rode his horse into the sea and shot
      a lady's fan off a pole on a Heike ship
('one of the most famous archery feats in Japanese history')

Noguchi, though, came here to Mure
for the stone – and it's easy to see why: dense,
compact, evenly granular, capable
of being polished to a perfectly smooth finish

       atelier, sculpture garden (unfinished works),
       exhibition space (finished works), house, garden,
       landscaped hillside with a view over the Inland Sea

a town inhabited by sculptors and stonecutters:
some manufacture granite statuettes
        of Snow White and the Seven Dwarfs
a few try their hand at Noguchi-style abstracts, but
the local speciality is gravestones

*

a sunny Tuesday in Tokyo

cat Suzunari is outside, sniffing at things on the balcony

strong warm winds from the south

the dreamy Japanese spring

Tokyo, Kamakura, Kobe, Takamatsu: January–March 2019

LOQUITUR

what you read is what you get

        (a belated imagist's logbook?
        a cheerful post-Whalen sprawl?
        a chronicle of fugaceous sensations?
        an episodic metropolitan renga?
        a handscroll moment-by-moment unrolled?
        wheelbarrow? rain water? chickens?)

perhaps not (tort law):

        res ipsa loquitur – 'the thing speaks for itself'

                ('an accident of a kind that does not
                ordinarily occur in the absence of negligence')

but (stage direction):

        loquitur – 'begins to speak'

                                what you get is what you hear

TEMPLE GARDEN

here

to sit
where

sitting
has been

valid

(voluble bulbul in a cypress tree)

TEMPLE, WORKMEN, CRANE, LARGE ROCK

place

the

rock

overgrown with ancient mosses

so that

it has been

here

for ever

BUSON'S DEER, ISSA'S RAIN, CHIYO'S FROG

1

calling three times
then to be heard no more
the deer in the rain

2

quiet rain falling in spring
long-lasting rain in May
light rain between the end of autumn and the start of winter
fine rain like mist
rain that falls heavily but soon clears
rain that falls in large drops
cooling rain that falls on a summer evening

rain dripping from straw-thatched eaves

3

crouching
peering up at the clouds
a frog

EP: *Thrones, Drafts & Fragments*

I

White-bearded, wearing his signature dark overcoat and hat, walking slowly with his stick, the poet shows me around the penultimate volume of his epic.

It isn't a book, though, it's a room: museum-like, irregularly shaped, with dim lighting, dark corners and alcoves, full of glass cases containing mummies and grave goods of extraordinary magnificence.

The poet, silent, leads me from exhibit to exhibit, occasionally pointing out a detail with his stick. The overall impression is one of incomparable splendour. But, after all's said and done, these are, of course, dead bodies.

2

After long silence, the poet at last reveals the concluding volume of his work. It isn't a book, though, it's a train: he conducts me to a seat in one of the carriages.

The journey isn't long. The track runs through suburban housing, then along a shopping street with a bank on every corner. We pass several Renaissance palazzi and glimpse across a canal a row of restored mediaeval houses painted in pristine colours.

The train enters a park whose main feature is a temple set back against – perhaps even carved out of – a rock face. It's unfinished, encased in scaffolding and swathed in protective sheets.

I then realise that the railway tracks ran out some distance before we reached this point, and the train is now immobilised, sunk to its axles in sand.

The weather's halcyon, the light clear and haunting.

There's no obvious way back.

THE SANDPIT TRAP

1

An ant scrabbles to climb out of a conical sandpit, a trap whose sides
     slope at exactly the critical angle of repose.
Sand trickles down from the lip, causing the ant to slip backwards,
     down towards the hole at the bottom of the pit, where the
     percolating grains sift into the open jaws of the void.

2

The fear is that unmasking the self will lead to complete loss of self:
     there is nothing but the mask, and the mask is covering a void.

3

What would happen, though, if self did fall through the hole?
A squirming annihilation?
An explosive self-combustion?
A transformation to diamond-like transcendence?
Perfect non-existence like that before existence and non-existence
     were ever thought of?

4

Let's start again from the beginning.
The ant, a perceiving agent in dialogue with its environment and its
     fellows, makes its way across the forest floor. Attentive to seed
     and fallen leaf, to pheromone and to the scent of fungus, the
     ant and its companions steer well clear of the ant lion's pit.
Just beneath humus and thin topsoil, and just beyond the range of
     creaturely hearing, the void meanwhile continues to sound its
     single note – the endlessly reverberating silence of an unstruck
     gong.

ORPHEUS

stand for an interval now at the head
of these stone stairs
winding up from the root of darkness

there it is, the sky:
bands of palest blues and faintest greys
ruffled cream, a wash of lemon yellow

down among the shadows, in depths
beyond river and boatman,
music was played that could salve all ills

so step out now, out into the world,
not looking back, and wait
under the open sky for her arrival

wait until you know
that she never even began the ascent
that she could not, and never can, follow

that the stain on daylight of
her absence
is not to be charmed away with lyre or song

THE PLEASURES OF PEACE

1

Sirens wail and steel objects fall from the sky,
giving banks and insurance offices heart attacks, axe-blow spasms
        that shrug masonry off its foundations –
building after building climbing down itself into the street
to be consumed in fire.

This happened before I was born, but as a child, peering
through gaps in wobbly wire-and-picket fencing, I saw
ruined cellars and shattered brickwork,
tattered wallpaper adorning ghost rooms two storeys up,
traces of vanished stairways climbing propped-up walls,
and lakes of rosebay willow herb – sheets of ruffled purple
mantling the rubble and bared earth of basements opened to sky.

2

When a fire or other disturbance opens up the ground, the seeds
of *Chamaenerion angustifolium* germinate. Some areas can, after
burning, be covered with dense stands of this species; in Britain in
the 1940s the plant became known as 'bombweed' due to its rapid
colonisation of the bomb craters.

3

Seventy and more years on, the trees on Hampstead Heath
heave their shoulders and rustle their spreading limbs like giants
        doing Tai Chi.
A sudden alarm call, and an unseen blackbird thrashes away through
        the heavy summer foliage.

Lifting its head above a bed of brambles, a single purple flower
stirs and sways, attentive
to the fleeting motions of the wind.

Among trees, across grass, through bracken, skirting thickets,
the path leads on like a thought.

A VISIT TO RUNMARÖ

in memory of Tomas Tranströmer

the ferry
backs carefully away from the landing stage
in a frothy swirl

and then the water settles

skerries   wooden jetties
the road
rises gently from foreshore to forest

I swallow the silence-potion

pine   silver birch   rowan
a red house where a crowd of ferns
has quietly advanced all the way to the doorstep

gravel-surfaced, the road winds
through forest, marsh and meadow
past school, chapel and graveyard

and now here's the poet's name
handwritten on a green mailbox at a junction
where a modest track leads off through trees
towards a steep slope down to the stony shore

'there it is,' says the old lady walking her dog
pointing to a small two-storey house

pale blue shingle walls
windows outlined in darker blue
red-tiled roof with a red-brick chimney
all placed on a platform of patient grey boulders

> *a house that senses*
> *the constellation of nails that holds its walls together*

garden chairs are stacked on the porch;
the house is quiet, keeps itself to itself;
behind the glass of the living room window
a dangle of wind chimes hangs motionless
as though waiting for someone to return

I walk back through forest
past scattered houses, past meadows
past a reed-fringed lake

> *the earth is springy under my feet*
> *and I suddenly understand that plants are thinking*

at the jetty, half an hour to wait for the boat

Runmarö, 15 August 2019

WEST

darkly rippling water bears up
a hundred moored yachts in the marina

a gust of wind, and the rigging strikes up a music:
a whistling, whining, thrumming, pitch-shifting drone,
and a gamelan-like
multifarious clinking of halyards on masts

*

at the bow of the ferry – passing between
Breakwater Fort and
Picklecombe Battery (now 103 desirable residences) –
burly, in shorts and T-shirt, a long scar on his chin:

> *Birmingham, terrible place, I live there*
> *ninety-seven per cent of the people in my part are Muslims*
> *scumbags the lot of them*
> *I've just been banned from Facebook for eighty-four days*
> *you can write about any religion you like*
> *but you can't say a word about Muslims*
> *I like it down here, Devon and Cornwall*
> *not like Birmingham, which is shit and full of scumbags*
> *you don't get any of that here*
> *I used to come on holiday down here when I was a boy*

sun and cloud,
        spray sheets in over the gunwale,
choppy seas to Cawsand, where
he doesn't disembark but heads straight back to Plymouth –
an appointment with a fortune teller at twelve o'clock

*

gangplank onto shingle
stone steps up to a café terrace

warm sun, cool breeze,
        waves splash on the pebbly beach
by the bluff dividing Cawsand from Kingsand

filigree balconies
        face out across the sound
from white- and cream-painted cottages
clustered below a massive grey stone fort's
emplacements. loopholes and embrasures

        salts and gunners supplanted now
        by yacht-owners jaunty in their sailor caps

cloud shadows and patches of sunlight
chase each other across the white-flecked sea

in the big sky above the fort
a stream of weather
funnels up from the farthest end of Cornwall

*

from the village square
        (postbox and war memorial)
past the Rising Sun with its cheery sign –
        Helios smiling down
        on meadow, river, a rooster perched on a post –
to a red gravel path traversing an open field

then woodland, woodland, woodland
mixed stands, mature trees
shifting and stirring in the wind from the west

to Mount Edgcumbe,
   house destroyed in the blitz, rebuilt
   in its earliest, Tudor form

at the entrance to the Earl's garden
a pasty, a bottle of water, a bench under a tree beside
a life-size stone Artemis
        in sleeveless knee-length tunic
with full quiver and accompanying doe

*

the bus skirts the fence of the naval base
    the next sunny blustery day
and drops me at the Carew Arms –
but it's a further two-mile walk to the house
by road, forest path and formal lime tree avenue

    (crackles, bangs, thumps and jolts
    clouds of smoke float
    above the trees on the southern horizon –
       practice firing at HMS *Raleigh*)

but here it is:
a four-square eighteenth-century building
full of portraits of ancestors and associates

Richard Carew of Antony
    author of *The Survey of Cornwall* (1602)
has his portrait (*pictor ignotus*) in the hall
Ætatis fuæ 32, *Ann° Dñi*, 1586

lightly bearded, hairline receding (*baldness, he concluded, was
a sign of imagination*), ears big, formally clothed in black,
holding a book tagged *invita morte vita* (life in spite of death)

> but looking
> more wary, more ascetic
> less lively, less waggish
> > (he wrote, after all, *A Herrings Tayle,*
> > a comic version of Sidney's *Arcadia*)
> less confident than expected

> > *his neglect the result of his own modesty, the re-
> > moteness of his dwelling, and the multitude of his
> > great contemporaries in and about the capital,
> > and not of any lack of merit*

Latin as a schoolboy, Oxford at eleven
Greek, German, Dutch, French, Spanish and Italian
(did he ever learn Cornish?)

> > *he ever delighted so much in reading for – if he had none
> > other hindrance – going or riding he would ever have a
> > book and be reading*

from the hall
> enter the library:
leather-bound volumes, dating back centuries,
or clothbound, late-Victorian or Edwardian:

> Thackeray's *Works* (twenty-four volumes)
> Major-General Sir Frederick Maurice KCB, *A History of the
> > War in South Africa* 1899–1902 (four volumes)
> Field Marshall Lord Roberts, *Forty-One Years in India* (two
> > volumes)
> Meyer's *British Birds* (seven volumes)

next door, in the wood-panelled, chandeliered 'saloon'
hardbacks in dust wrappers on coffee tables
Wolf Hall and *Bring Up the Bodies* –
and someone's reading *Swallows and Amazons*

      upstairs, in the Porch Bedroom:
      floor to ceiling
      nineteenth-century portraits
      of the master's horses and dogs

outside, a lawn leads down to a creek
      (a Brunel viaduct in the distance)
where, from rubber boats, trainees are boarding
a small grey warship moored mid-channel

   *

six raids, spring 1941
      six hundred dead and thousands injured
(Auntie Belle a nurse at the Prince of Wales Hospital)

schools and churches
      Guildhall, post office, thousands of houses
(Grandma could see the flames from St Merryn, forty miles away)

      summer 1941: roads through acres of rubble

      out of the disasters of war to snatch
      a victory for the city of the future

A PLAN FOR PLYMOUTH
      (by Canberra out of New Delhi)
dropped in one piece onto the flattened city

*with the return of 'community' will come the spirit of
companionship unknown to the youth of yesterday who
vainly sought it in the car or the cinema*

Armada Way –
            boulevard from station to Hoe –
where homeless sleepers in the doorways lie
and street lights blanch the midnight sky

*a year or two of uncertainty, but then we'll be all right
we've done it before, after the war, so we'll do it again*

(24 June 2016)

*absolutely delighted
very proud to be British this morning
we're going to stand alone again*

some pointed looks at Maya
down by the harbour-side pubs

at the B&B the landlady is watching
the Westminster debates on TV
*it's getting ridiculous!
they seem to have forgotten there was a vote!*

*

from the small station at St Germans, Quay Road leads
downhill to stone buildings and a grassy wharf,
once busy with timber, coal and limestone

white yachts rest their hulls on low-tide mud
in late afternoon sunlight

silence
        except when a train
rumbles over Brunel's high-arched viaduct

beyond which, Old Quay Road climbs back up
to the village
to the part-Norman abbey
        (once seat of the Cornish bishopric)
to the crenellated neo-Gothic gate to Port Eliot

all these great houses!
        Mount Edgcumbe, Antony, Port Eliot, Cotehele
and all these grand families:

> *a gentleman and his wife will ride to make merry with his*
> *next neighbour, and after a day or twain those two couples go*
> *to a third, in which progress they increase like snowballs, till*
> *through their burdensome weight they break again*

Richard Carew's vanished Elizabethan world

but their descendants are
still energetic, still making ends meet
        (Mount Edgcumbe's family-friendly attractions –
                Baba Yaga's Circus, Flyers Disc Golf, Archery Assault
                wild swimming, paddleboard, kayak and canoe)
still in full possession –
        cultural, psychological, social, economic –
of inherited assets, privileges and entitlements

the recent portraits in their hallways:
tall, handsome, vigorous, competent
military-looking men and their glamorous wives

*

(interlude)

language on display
at the eco-lit conference in Plymouth:

situated knowledge

    late catapultism

        counter-desecration

           the after-normal

    the Anthroposcenic

              (end of interlude)

*

across the Tamat, heading west by train
through the green, rounded
landscape of south-east Cornwall,
Brunel's track curving
on viaducts over mud-flat creeks
or above the deep, steep valleys –
I know every childhood inch of this –
and on through woods to Bodmin Road –

sorry, Bodmin Parkway, the station name
changed more than thirty years ago

*

Hepworth's studio and garden at Trewyn
        her atelier with its anthology of shapes –
carved, smoothed, harp-strung, polished

        the strings were the tension I felt between
        myself and the sea, the wind or the hills

white-frame glass-roof workshops among
tall bamboos, palm trees,
mosses, ferns and succulents

        the rocky hills, fertile valleys and dynamic coastline
        provided me with a background and a soil

grey stone, chisel-flecked or polished –
or the pleasures of patina, pools
        of rainwater in bronze concavities
shining, rippling, reflecting plants and sky

        here is sufficient field for exploration to last a lifetime

the small white shed with its narrow
bed for naps and early starts in summer

    (immediately before her death
    fifteen tons of Carrara marble were delivered
    and placed in the yard
    waiting to be carved *like a flock of patient sheep*)

it would be possible to carve the same subject in a different
stone each time, throughout life, without a repetition of form

*

Nicholson, Lanyon, Barns-Graham
Frost, Heron, Hilton, Wynter and Wells

good for the eyes
    good to see the actual paint
        again, even if by now
less shock of the new

    long ago
    taken to heart and
    photographed by an inward eye

Porthmeor sea light refracted through curved glass
ripples on the ceiling

*

in the Tate shop
they've never heard of W. S. Graham

        (a long time since I last was here …)

new nameplates beside cottage doors
        (italic script carved in slate)
'hospitality' companies
snappers-up of whatever came on the market

the town bookshop has survived
the second-hand booksellers gone

        one gallery (only) not
        specialising in souvenir seascapes

I buy an ice cream
        (Kelly's: childhood memories)
a gull dive-bombs me for it

*

a few surfers on Porthmeor Beach
        (not much swell this morning)
lifeguards amble about, setting up flags for the day

a gentle breeze, sun on my face
I sit on a bench high on a grassy slope facing the Atlantic
sea splashes on granite
seagulls sit on lichened rocks
an occasional small fishing boat chugs past

below me a kestrel
hovers, swoops to
adjust its field of
observation, hovers
again, head
immobile, wings
vibrating, every mottle
of its pinions
limned, its tail
feathers spread in a
splayed triangle, then

stoops to the hillside –
        a small high scream –
claws extended to kill

*

7:00 a.m., leaving St Ives in pouring rain

the bus company man in the bus company office
sits in front of the bus company fire

        – do you have a waiting room?
        – no
        – may we shelter in here?
        – no
        – is there anywhere to shelter nearby?
        – no
        – nowhere?
        – nothing to do with me, mate

*

Penzance to the Isles of Scilly
choppy seas, rainy weather, wind force 4 or 5
         12,000 years ago we could have walked it
         oak, ash and hazel, red deer, wild boar

Hughtown – a substantial harbour,
         substantial rows of granite houses –
looks like a garrison town – which is what it was:

         gun platforms, star castle, bastions and batteries
         from 1593 to World War II
                  holding the western approaches
         against Spanish, Dutch, French or Germans

the sky clears, dinner by the harbour
beside the quick-ruffled, restless, whitecapped sea

*

open boat under a serene blue sky
between low-lying, twin-hilled islands

         wobbly gangplank onto
         a beach at Bryher

fine sand, emerald and turquoise water,
         small boats bob and clink at anchor

across the sound
King Charles's ruined hilltop castle and –
         dressed granite,
                  severe, cylindrical, functional –
Cromwell's Castle by the water's edge

once the royalists had been ejected (1651)
        by Robert Blake, General at Sea
loyal protestants were shipped in
and settled –
                which must be why these islands
which I thought might be more Cornish than Cornwall
seem so English

*in the late seventeenth century visitors often commented on how
cosmopolitan and well-spoken the islanders were, a stark contrast
to the people of West Cornwall, many of whom spoke only Cornish*

        the road on St Martins goes from
        Highertown to Lowertown via Middletown

on Bryher the main settlement is called The Town

*

path through bracken above the sea
the *slip-slop-sshhh*
                of small waves
the only sound

sandy tracks, short turf, a reed-edged pool,
deep swell pluming white
        on distant offshore rocks,
Hell's Bay a cauldron of restless water

narrow rectangular fields –
        agapanthus, lilies, daffodils, cabbages –
high (four- or five-metre) bushy windbreak hedges

cormorant, sandpiper, tern, curlew, kittiwake
egret, fulmar, gannet, oystercatcher
ringed plover, grey heron, shag and turnstone

*

approaching Cornwall
the ship
mounts, heaves, shivers and slithers through the swell

    the Minack Theatre
              on the cliff at Porthcurno, where
    I first saw *The Tempest* fifty-odd years ago
    barely visible in the mist

Penzance
as we draw near
swathed in a grey veil of rain

4–12 *September* 2019

ON THE TRAIN TO WORCESTER

wet stubble beside the track
waterlogged paths through swampy fields
autumnal sunlight on
       autumnal trees reflected in
            lakes of autumnal floodwater
a caravan in a damp
back garden, yellow leaves strewn on grass,
tall cypresses and an aluminium chimney

the train moves forward at a steady pace
the eye gazes out, the local pours past the window
the mind makes its edits
what doesn't get framed won't have been seen

only 3:00 p.m. and it's nearly evening!

      low light inundates the Severn valley
      sheep cast long shadows on cropped grass

tattered clouds
half a mile of longboats moored on a dark canal
a red-streaked rainy sunset up ahead

a pair of pheasants
flap away from the passing train in alarm

13 *November* 2019

Notes, Sources, Thanks

Passages: Poems 1969–2019 includes most of the poems from five retrospective collections and two gatherings of new work published by Isobar Press between 2013 and 2021, together with two poems that only ever appeared in *In Daylight,* and some pages from *Monumenta Nipponica,* both published in 1995. The poems are in roughly chronological order; some have been revised, and in a few cases have been given new titles; some poems from the individual volumes have been omitted, and a few entirely new pieces have been added.

§

'Notes', said Basil Bunting, 'are a confession of failure' – before proceeding to include six pages of them at the back of his *Collected Poems.* Some poets are stricter with themselves than Bunting was, and on principle provide no notes at all; others, such as Marianne Moore and William Empson, provide long, even garrulous – and often very interesting – annotations to their poems. *Passages* tries to follow a middle course. Three types of annotation are included: citations of sources that poems allude to, or adopt or adapt language from; some names, historical facts, and words in various languages (mostly Japanese) that readers might not know; and a few pieces of information that I simply found interesting enough to want to relay – the catastrophic scale of the population decline in eighth-century China, for example. I hope the notes in all three categories might be useful or enjoyable or both.

Japanese names are in the Japanese order, with family name first, except in the case of Japanese authors who have mostly worked and published in English.

NOTES TO THE POEMS

BASHŌ

Variations on Matsuo Bashō's *Genjuan no Fu* ('Prose Poem on the Unreal Dwelling'), based on Donald Keene's English translation of it in his *Anthology of Japanese Literature: From the Earliest Era to the Mid-Nineteenth Century*.

READING THE T'ANG POETS IN TOKYO, 1969

The lines in italics are from Po Chü-i (Hakurakuten in Japanese), 'Playing the Lute in the Cool of the Evening'; see R. H. Blyth, *Haiku Volume 1: Eastern Culture*, for a (very different) translation of the complete poem. For what the T'ang poets in general had seen, see the note below on Tu Fu's 'Seeing Kung Sun's Pupil Dance'. Po Chü-i lived a little later than Tu Fu, after peace had – relatively speaking – been restored, although there continued to be rebellions and insurrections throughout his lifetime.

IN THE MOUNTAINS: FOUR POEMS

The title of the third poem is adapted from the last line of Gary Snyder's 'Hymn to the Goddess San Francisco in Paradise', published in *Six Sections from Mountains and Rivers Without End* in 1965 but later excluded from the completed *Mountains and Rivers* sequence.

ON TREVOSE HEAD

William Rossiter was born in Plymouth in 1853, served as an able (later, leading) seaman on various Royal Navy ships, including the *Osprey*-class sloop HMS *Wild Swan*, which took part in anti-slavery operations in Mozambique in 1881; he later became a coastguard and from 1901 to 1903 was stationed at Trevose Head in St Merryn, Cornwall. He and his wife Emma had six children, of whom Edwin, my grandfather (born 1894), was the second youngest.

CROSSING THE PASS

The last two lines are from Hui Neng (638–713), the sixth Zen patriarch, spoken to settle a dispute between two monks.

Ken Wall was artist-in-residence at the Brewery Arts Centre in Kendal, Cumbria, in the mid-1970s.

THE TEMPTATION OF SAINT ANTHONY

The painting is the Bosch workshop copy in the Musée des Beaux Arts in Bruxelles.

SEEING KUNG-SUN'S PUPIL DANCE

A translation done with the help of David Hawkes's *A Little Primer of Tu Fu*. The 'disturbances' mentioned in the introduction were the 'An-Shi Disturbances', otherwise known as the An Lu-shan Rebellion, of 755–763. David Hinton in his biography of the poet in his *Selected Poems of Tu Fu* reports that, according to the official census, the population of China fell from 53 million before the rebellion to 17 million afterwards. That is, 36 million people died, were displaced, rendered homeless, or otherwise lost to view, during these few years, a figure that represents two-thirds of the population of the Chinese empire, or one-sixth of the population of the world, at that time.

WANG WEI WRITES A LETTER

Excerpted and adapted from a letter (in prose) from Wang Wei to his friend P'ei Ti. *Wang Wei: Poems,* translated by G. W. Robinson.

PARADEISOS

Figulus (Latin): a potter, a maker of earthenware goods.

CERNE ABBAS

The quotation in part 1 is from Strabo's *Geography*; the missionary in part 2 is St Augustine of Canterbury; the story about the cow's tail is told by William of Malmesbury. Part 5: recent research (2021), using 'optically stimulated luminescence testing', suggests that the Giant was originally created in the late Saxon era.

Part 1: Ben Jonson's version of Catullus VII in *The Forrest* (1616); Alexander Pope, *The Rape of the Lock,* (1712), Canto 1; William Blake, *Vala, or The Four Zoas* (1797–1807), 'Night the Second'. The refrain in part 4 is adapted from a line in James Michie's translation of Horace's *Carmen saeculare*; Blake's vision of angels on Peckham Rye is reported in Alexander Gilchrist's *Life of William Blake.* For most of the twentieth century the Lots Road power station in Chelsea supplied electricity for the London Underground, at its peak burning up to 700 tonnes of coal a day; Dungeness A on Romney Marsh was a generation-1 nuclear power station, producing electricity for the national grid and plutonium-239 for the British atomic weapons programme.

ALTITUDE

Nil mortalibus ardui est: 'nothing is too difficult (high, lofty) for humankind'.

DESERT SUN, WIND FROM THE NORTH

On 22 September 1980 the Iraqi army attacked the Iranian river port of Khorramshahr. By 10 November, after heavy shelling and fierce fighting, the Iraqis had gained control of the city, which they occupied until May 1982, when the Iranians retook it. The buzzards near the end of the poem are European and Middle-Eastern *Buteo* (large hawks) rather than the North American *Cathartes* (turkey vultures).

READING HORACE IN KUWAIT

The phrases in italics are adapted from James Michie's translation of Ode 1.22; the epigraph is translated in the first quotation in part 2.

THE FAVOURS

The Sura of the Beneficent, Koran XV, in Pickthal's translation.

PALEOPAPHOS

The epigraph ('Where love is, there is sight'): Richard of St Victor, quoted by Ezra Pound in Canto XC. The quotation in part 3 is from *The Odyssey* III.

The third set of Chinese characters in fact reads 'Itabashi Honcho', the name of a subway station in northern Tokyo; the quotations are from Abe Kōbō, *The Woman of the Dunes,* translated by E. Dale Saunders, and Jacques Derrida, 'Structure, Sign, and Play' in *Writing and Difference,* translated by Alan Bass.

KOMACHI

Ōta Shōgo's *Komachi Fuden* ('Komachi as told by the wind') is a modern adaptation of the noh play *Sotoba Komachi* by Kan'ami Kiyotsugu (1333–84). The protagonist of both plays is Ono no Komachi, a Heian-period poet equally famous for her poetry, her beauty and her heartlessness. One suitor, Fukakusa no Shosho, was refused until he had completed a vigil outside her house every night for a hundred nights. He died on the ninety-ninth night, but when Komachi was an old woman, he came back to haunt her; the climax of Kan'ami's play is a dance in which she is seized by his spirit and dances out his passion and grief. Sotoba: a stupa (a structure marking a Buddhist grave).

STRAW AGAINST THE WINTER

Jizō is the bodhisattva Kshitigarbha, protector of travellers and children; small statues of him (often wearing a red bib) are frequently found beside roads and paths in Japan.

KOGŌ: SCENE 2

Kogō is a noh play by Komparu Zenchiku (1405–1468). The letter brought by Nakakuni is a love letter from the Emperor.

AIR

The epigraph is from John James, *A Theory of Poetry.*

BON-ODORI IN KABUKICHO

Bon-odori is the traditional dance of the festival of O-Bon, in which every August the spirits of the dead revisit the earth and are welcomed and entertained by their descendants. Kabukichō is a large red-light district in Tokyo.

BOW, CLAP TWICE, AND PRAY

The traditional manner of address to the spirit resident in a Shinto shrine.

THE WAY OF TEA

Sentences from *Chatei no Ki* (Teahouse Record) by Takuan Sōhō (1573–1645). The River Wei, north of the old Chinese capital, Chang'an, was noted – by Tu Fu among others – for its clear water.

KAGEKIYO

Based on a noh play attributed to Zeami Motokiyo (1363–1443); the complete play has been translated by both Ezra Pound and Arthur Waley. Kagekiyo was a captain of the Taira clan in the much-fabled Genpei War of 1180–85 between the Minamoto (Genji) and Taira (Heike) clans, a conflict narrated in the epic *Heike Monogatari* (The Tale of the Heike). After the defeat of the Taira, Kagekiyo is exiled to a remote area and lives as an old, blind beggar. His daughter, who is searching for him, comes to his hut by chance and asks for directions, but, ashamed of his state, he sends her away without revealing who he is. However, a villager brings her back, and father and daughter are briefly reunited. He agrees to tell her about his past as a warrior, but insists that after that his daughter leave him and return home.

HIROSHIMA

Part 1 quotes from the introduction to the catalogue accompanying a 1984 Hiroshima Peace Memorial Museum exhibition of art by survivors of the bombing; the words of two of these survivors are quoted at the end of Part 2 and in Part 3.

MONUMENTA NIPPONICA

The Japanese word *yoroshiku* is used for a variety of communicative purposes, among them greeting, bonding, and applying social pressure; English equivalents of some of these uses might be 'How do you do?', 'Please send my regards' and 'Please see to it'.

LANGUAGE ACQUISITION

Based on an incident reported by the linguist Patricia Clancy in 'The Acquisition of Communicative Style in Japanese,' in *Language Socialization Across Cultures*, ed. E. Schieffelin & E. Ochs.

POSEOKJEONG BOWER

The stone feature described in this poem is all that remains of the royal palace of the Unified Silla kingdom on the Korean peninsula. King Gyeong-ae Wang of Silla died here in 927 during an invasion by King Gyeonhwon of the rival Baekje kingdom; although Silla survived as a client state of Baekje until 935, Gyeong-ae Wang's death is usually seen as signalling the end of the kingdom.

THE KINGDOM OF PAGAN

The kingdom (in north Burma) lasted from 1044 to 1287. In the capital city of 200,000 inhabitants there were over 10,000 Buddhist temples and pagodas, of which more than 2,000 survive.

PAK WAYAN, SITTING ON THE VERANDA OF HIS LOSMEN

Wayan is a name often given to the eldest sibling in a Balinese family; Pak (father) is an honorific; a losmen is an inn or hostel. The last line is from an article about the Indonesian massacres of 1965 in *Time*, 17 December 1965.

THE BURIAL MASK

Based on motifs in George Seferis's 'The King of Asini' (1940). The poem has been translated in full by Bernard Spencer, Nanos Valaoritis and Lawrence Durrell (1948); Rex Warner (1960); and Edmund Keeley and Philip Sherrard (1967 / 1981 /1995).

FOR PESSOA

Versions of lines from several poems by Fernando Pessoa and two of his heteronyms, Ricardo Reis and Álvaro de Campos – especially the latter's 'Tobacconist's' and 'I Have a Terrible Cold' – adapted from Jonathan Griffin's translations in Fernando Pessoa, *Selected Poems*.

The introductory note is from Isabel Carlisle's pamphlet that accompanied the Joseph Beuys exhibition *The secret block for a secret person in Ireland* at the Royal Academy in London in 1999.

RAG-A-BONE

The poem includes quotations from *Alfred Wallis: Primitive* by Sven Berlin; it also incorporates a few phrases from W. S. Graham's poem 'The Voyages of Alfred Wallis'.

VENETIAN CASTLE: IRAKLION

The epigraph ('Peace to you, Mark, my evangelist; here your body will lie') was spoken by an angel to St Mark when he visited the lagoon where Venice would later be founded. In fact, his body was interred at Alexandria until 828 CE, when it was stolen by Venetian merchants and taken to Venice, whereupon the saint was adopted as the city's patron. The quotation in part 2 is from Desreaux de Richardière, *Voyage de Candie Fait Par l'Armée de France en l'Année 1669* (Paris, 1671), quoted by John Julian Norwich in his *A History of Venice*.

KNOSSOS

Sir Arthur Evans (1851–1941) was the chief excavator of the Minoan palace complex at Knossos in Crete; he began in the 1920s to use modern materials in an attempt to create a facsimile of the palace based on his interpretation of the archaeological evidence he had found.

ARKADI

The Orthodox monastery of Arkadi, built in the sixteenth century, was a major centre in the Cretan Revolt of 1866, and was stormed by the Turkish army on 8–9 November of that year. Of the 943 people inside the monastery at the beginning of the assault, 846 were killed; about 1,500 of the 15,000 Turkish troops also died.

Angelos Sikelianos' Greek text is twice as long as this minimalist version, which is loosely based on Edmund Keeley and Philip Sherrard's English translation of the complete poem.

ELYSIUM BRITANNICUM

Phrases from a review by Keith Thomas of John Ingram's edition of *Elysium Britannicum, or The Royal Gardens* by John Evelyn in the *London Review of Books* 20.4 (July 2001). The second and third sections are chapter titles for lost parts of Evelyn's work; the lines in italics are quotations from Evelyn.

A SHORT NARRATIVE OF THE RESTAURATION OF HIS MAJESTY

John Aubrey, *Brief Lives*, edited by Oliver Lawson Dick, mainly the Lives of James Harrington (1611–77), republican theorist and author of *Oceana*, and George Monk (1608–70), Commander-in-Chief of the Army in Scotland, plus one quotation from Aubrey ('his Majestie and his Royal Highnesse…') found in Anthony Powell, *John Aubrey and His Friends*.

THE CORNISH HEDGE

Part 1 includes information from the Cornwall Council website; the rest of the piece is adapted from passages in Sarah Carter's twenty-five year diary of a mile of hedge near her home in the West Penwith area of Cornwall, 'The Life and Death of a Flailed Cornish Hedge', the Cornish Hedges Library, www.cornishhedges.co.uk/papers.htm

AUGUST LINES

Fulcit Atlanteo rupes ea vertice caelos: Andrew Marvell's Latin poem on Almscliff Crag and Bilborough, 'Epigramma in Duos Montes Amosclivium et Bilboreum', was written in the 1650s at Appleton House in Wharfedale.

READING PHILIP WHALEN

Quotations from Philip Whalen, *Memoirs of an Interglacial Age* and *Severance Pay*, and Michael McClure, *Scratching the Beat Surface* .

RECOMMENDING TRISTANO

Richard Cook and Brian Morton, *The Penguin Guide to Jazz Recordings*; Larry Kart, liner notes to *The Complete Atlantic Recordings of Lennie Tristano, Lee Konitz & Warne Marsh* (Mosaic, 1997); J. Bradford Robinson, article on Tristano in *The New Grove Dictionary of Jazz* (1994); Barry Ulanov, liner notes to *The New Tristano* (Atlantic, 1961).

KNOWING ONE'S PLACE

Setagaya is a residential area in south Tokyo. Setagaya Castle, seat of the Kira clan, was destroyed in 1590 by Toyotomi Hideyoshi after his defeat of the Hōjō clan, with whom the Kira were allied, at the siege of Odawara. At Sekigahara in 1600 the successors of Hideyoshi were in turn defeated by Tokugawa Ieyasu in a battle that established him as undisputed ruler of Japan; the rule of his family lasted until the Meiji Restoration of 1868. The treaty signed by Ii Naosuke was an unequal one, opening Japanese ports and granting extraterritorial privileges to American citizens, hence the resentment of it.

KNOWING ONE'S PLACE: PART 2

The first quotation is from an eighteenth-century official of the Bakufu (shogunate). For Hideyoshi, see the previous note. Until the Meiji Restoration in 1868 only aristocrats and samurai were allowed to have family names.

VISITING THE ANCESTORS

Okonomiyaki: a savoury pancake containing a variety of ingredients; NHK, the Japanese national broadcasting corporation; 'haafu' (half): Japanese English for a person of mixed race. The Heike (also known as the Taira) were one of the clans fighting for control of Japan in the Genpei war of 1180–85, a struggle recounted in the epic *Heike Monogatari* (The Tale of the Heike), in which the death of Taira no Atsumori is one of the most famous episodes. Dera: temple; sakaki: a sacred evergreen plant.

LOOKING AT THE CITY FROM PARLIAMENT HILL

Quotation in part 2: a human resources specialist talking to Joris Luyendijk over a glass of Haut Poitou Sauvignon Blanc; *The Guardian*, 2 November 2011.

The Survey of Cornwall, by Richard Carew of Antony (1602): the 1769 edition (using the original spelling) is available online at archive.org. I have modernised *u/v* and *i/j* spellings. Crowning: conducting a coroner's inquest; stickleness: roughness, difficulty; gayle: gaol; planching: floorboards; mazer: a wooden bowl or cup.

THE INVENTION OF THE LAKE DISTRICT

Thomas Gray, *Journal of His Visit to the Lake District*. Gray visited the Lake District in 1769. His companion, Dr Thomas Wharton, who had asthma, dropped out early in the journey; Gray continued on his own and kept a journal for the benefit of his friend. The 'glass' in part 2 is a Claude glass; see part 2 of 'The Poetry of Place' on pages 366–7. The quotation in part 3 is from Dante (*Inferno* 3.1.51): 'Let us not speak of them; but look and pass on.'

PIET MONDRIAN IN BELSIZE PARK

Mondrian's letters are extensively quoted by Charles Darwent in *Mondrian in London: How British Art Nearly Became Modern*. Mondrian left from Liverpool for New York on 23 September 1940.

DIFFERENCE & REPETITION

John Wylie, 'A Single Day's Walking: Narrating Self and Landscape on the South West Coast Path', *Transactions of the Institute of British Geographers, NS* 30, 2005.

SEA-CHANGE

'*The Tempest* deals in compound words … flung together and left to work out their complex and unstable union within the reader's mind.' (Ann Barton).

BUSON'S DEER, ISSA'S RAIN, CHIYO'S FROG

Issa's rain: Arran Stibbe, *Ecolinguistics: Language, Ecology and the Stories We Live By*; Buson's deer and Chiyo's frog: Stephen Addis, Fumiko Yamamoto and Akira Yamamoto, *A Haiku Menagerie: Living Creatures In Poems And Prints*.

The language in italics consists of slightly modified versions of lines from 'Along the Lines (Far North)', 'A Winter Night', and 'Schubertiana' in Tomas Tranströmer, *The Half-Half-Finished Heaven: Selected Poems,* translated by Robert Bly. Runmarö is the island in the Stockholm Archipelago where Tomas Tranströmer spent his summers.

WEST

Oliver Garnett, *Antony*, National Trust Guide (2002); F. E. Halliday, 'Richard Carew: A Cornish Gentleman in the Age of Elizabeth I', *History Today* 3.3 (March 1953); Patrick Abercrombie and J. Paton Watson, *A Plan for Plymouth* (1943); 'The People of Plymouth's Reaction to Brexit', *ITV News*, 24 June 2016; Barbara Hepworth, 'Texts', http://barbarahepworth.org.uk/; Neil Reid, *Isles of Scilly Guidebook.*

THANKS

I'm enormously grateful to the publishers of my first three books: Matthew Zuckerman for *In Daylight* (Printed Matter Press, 1995); the late Drew Stroud / Ryu Makoto for *Monumenta Nipponica* (Saru Press, 1995); and Peter Robinson for the original edition of *The Painting Stick* (Pine Wave Press, 2005).

Some poems included here have appeared in recent years in print or online journals – sincere thanks to all the editors concerned: David Caddy (*Tears in the Fence*), James Crocker (*The Font*), Tony Frazer and Kelvin Corcoran (*Shearsman*), Michael Glover (*The Bow Wow Shop*), Wolfgang Görtschacher (*Poetry Salzburg Review*), Taylor Mignon (*Tokyo Poetry Journal*), Ban'ya Natsuishi (*Ginyu* and *World Haiku*), the late Ken Rodgers (*Kyoto Journal*), Lou Rowan *(Golden Handcuffs Review),* Philip Rowland (NOON: *journal of the short poem*), Michael Schmidt (*PN Review*), Aidan Semmens (*Molly Bloom*), and Gary Young (*Otoliths*). 'Reading Philip Whalen' appeared online in *A Festschrift for Tony Frazer*, and three pieces from 'En Route' were printed in *jar of rain: The Red Moon Anthology of English-Language Haiku 2020* (Red Moon Press); thanks to Richard Berengarten at al. for the former, and to Jim Kacian for the latter.

A number of Tokyo friends have over the years read and commented very helpfully on my poems: Arthur Binard, Chris Cleary, Tom Dow, the late Denis Doyle, John Evans, Andrew Fitzsimons, John Gribble, Lesley Hardy, Philip Rowland, and Matthew Zuckerman. Warm thanks to all.

Last – but definitely not least – I'm most grateful to all the poets and translators who have entrusted their work to Isobar Press since 2013, and from whom I've learned so much.